EFFECTIVE

How Can We Best Help Others?

Dedicated to David Pearce

CONTENTS

PREFACE

Two meanings of the term "effective altruism" are worth distinguishing: effective altruism as the ideal of helping others as much as possible, and effective altruism as a social movement consisting of people who are trying to live up to this ideal. This book is about effective altruism in the first sense: it seeks to examine and reflect on how we can best help others. It does not speak for the entire effective altruism community, nor could it. Indeed, no one person can speak for a community with such diverse views as the effective altruism community. Yet that should not prevent any member of this community, or indeed anyone else, from publicly examining the ideal of effective altruism — examining and reflecting on what helping others as much as possible means and entails. On the contrary, such critical examination seems necessary to advance ourselves toward a more well-considered understanding of the ideal of effective altruism.

As an examination of this ideal, this book should provide food for thought both to people who have never heard the term "effective altruism", as well as to those who think about effective altruism every day.

INTRODUCTION: WHAT IS EFFECTIVE ALTRUISM?

"[…] effective altruism is the project of using evidence and reason to figure out how to benefit others as much as possible, and taking action on that basis."

— William MacAskill[1]

Effective altruism is all about taking maximal advantage of our enormous opportunity to improve the world. It is about using our limited resources to help sentient beings as much as we can.

There are two core elements to effective altruism. First, there is the altruism itself. This is not altruism in the irresponsible sense of sacrificing for others without any regard for oneself, but rather in the simple sense of improving the lives of others — something that requires us to take very good care of ourselves indeed. This may be considered the emotional part of effective altruism. The burning flame at the center that animates the project. Second, there is the effectiveness. This is the cooler, more cerebral aspect that asks us to optimize our core goal: helping other sentient beings is great, but helping them as much as our resources allow is even greater.

---

[1] MacAskill, 2017.

In this way, effective altruism is a project that requires us to combine both the heart and the head; empathy and evidence; compassion and careful consideration.

Singer's Shallow Pond

A thought experiment often used to introduce the motivation behind effective altruism is Peter Singer's shallow pond argument. The situation is this: you are walking past a shallow pond in which a child is drowning, and you can save the child if you are willing to jump in the pond and have your clothes and shoes ruined. The question Singer then asks us is: should you jump in the pond and save the child?

This can almost seem like a trick question, as the answer seems an all too obvious "yes". Yet what if there are other people around the pond besides you who could also save the child, but who choose not to? That would not seem to change much: most of us agree we should still save the child. Imagine, then, that the drowning child is not in a pond right next to you, but a full kilometer away, and imagine that you can still save the child by exercising the same amount of effort that would be required if the child were in a pond right next to you. Should you then still save the child? The answer, again, seems an obvious "of course". So too if the child were 100 kilometers away, or indeed on the other side of the planet, provided that the child can still be saved with the same low level of effort.

All of this can seem rather unremarkable: we have merely established the rather obvious proposition that we should save a child's life, regardless of where in the world the child is, if we can do so at a minimal cost to ourselves, such as the price of some clothes and a pair of shoes. Yet the point of Singer's argument is that the implications of accepting this proposition are in fact anything but trivial, since we, Singer argues, find ourselves in a similar situation right now:

[...] we are all in that situation of the person passing the shallow pond: we can all save lives of people, both children and adults, who would otherwise die, and we can do so at a very small cost to us: the cost of a new CD, a shirt or a night out at a restaurant or concert, can mean the difference between life and death to more than one person somewhere in the world – and overseas aid agencies like Oxfam overcome the problem of acting at a distance.[2]

So how can we defend not donating to charities that do such life saving work, given that we agree that saving someone's life is worth the price of some clothes and a pair of shoes? One may, of course, object that there is greater uncertainty in the case of organized charity, yet as Singer notes:

[...] even if a substantial proportion of our donations were wasted, the cost to us of making the donation is so small, compared to the benefits that it provides when it, or some of it, does get through to those who need our help, that we would still be saving lives at a small cost to ourselves – even if aid organizations were much less efficient than they actually are.[3]

Now, it should be noted that the specifics of this thought experiment have been criticized by many, including some self-identified effective altruists.[4] For instance, the price of saving a human life does not seem comparable to that of a CD, but appears to rather be in the thousands of dollars. Yet even

---

[2] Singer, 1997.

[3] Ibid.

[4] See for instance Sinick, 2013.

if critiques like this one hold true, Singer's argument still serves as a good starting point for our thinking about effective altruism. Irrespective of any particular criticism we may level at Singer's argument, the more general point still stands undisputed. We, as citizens of the world, have the potential to greatly help other individuals, likely a large number of them, with the time and money we have at our disposal, and many of us can do so without sacrificing anything of significant, much less comparable, value to ourselves. And the core question of effective altruism is how we can best realize this potential. That is the question this book seeks to examine.

A Brief Note on Ethics

Before venturing into a deeper examination of this question, it is worth visiting two other questions, the first one being: why be an effective altruist? The short answer, which I believe satisfies most aspiring effective altruists,[5] is implicit in the considerations above. In the simplest of terms: for the same reason that we think we should save the child in the shallow pond (why we should be altruists), and because saving more individuals from suffering and premature death is, other things being equal, better than saving fewer individuals (why we should be *effective* altruists). For those who do not find this answer satisfying, my own attempt to provide a fuller answer is found in my book *You Are Them*.[6]

The second question is whether effective altruism is just a rebranding of utilitarianism, the ethical theory that we should maximize the well-

---

[5] From this point onward, I shall simply refer to "aspiring effective altruists" as "effective altruists", as it becomes too wordy otherwise. Yet I do think it is important to keep the "aspiring" in mind, as that is both a more accurate and rightfully humble description.

[6] A book that also explains why, in my view, "effective altruism" ultimately is a misnomer. Really, it is "effective egoism"/"effective selfishness", in the most sensible, albeit not usual, sense of these terms.

being of sentient beings. And the short answer to this question is "no". For although utilitarianism implies that we should be effective altruists, at least of some kind, the arrow does not point the other way. That is, one can be an effective altruist without being a utilitarian.[7] For instance, one can be an ethical pluralist who ascribes value to a wide variety of things, where helping others effectively with one's surplus resources is one of them. Indeed, one can be a full-fledged deontologist or virtue ethicist[8] and consider effective altruism a natural consequence of these views too. For instance, one may consider it a duty to follow the rule "try to help others effectively with your surplus resources", or consider efforts to help others in this way an essential part of a virtuous life.

Having visited these questions, let us now proceed in our examination of how to best help others. We shall begin with some groundwork.

---

[7] This looser character of effective altruism compared to utilitarianism is probably in large part what explains its much broader appeal (along with the better name).

[8] Deontology, or duty ethics, refers to a class of ethical theories that hold that we should always act according to certain rules — e.g. Immanuel Kant was a deontologist who thought we should always act according to the rule "do not lie" — while virtue ethics, mostly associated with Aristotle, holds that we should try to be as virtuous as possible, e.g. embody virtues such as modesty, honesty, discipline, and compassion as well as we can in our daily lives.

THE CORE VIRTUES OF
EFFECTIVE ALTRUISM

Before we ask how we can maximize our potential to help others, we must first get our minds ready and open for doing so. This we shall do by reviewing some ideas and thinking tools that play a crucial role in the pursuit of effective altruism; one could even say they are its defining virtues.

It Is an Open Question

The first and most foundational of these virtues is to admit that the question concerning how we can best help other individuals really is a question. And an extremely open and complex one at that. This may seem obvious, yet our attempts to improve the world nonetheless rarely reflect this openness and complexity. Most people have their own ideas about how to best improve the world — e.g. "ending fracking", or "converting everyone to the One True God" — yet few seem to have reflected critically upon these ideas, as opposed to just participating in a cultural echo choir. This should not be a surprise, as we did not evolve to ask and think deeply about questions of this nature, much less come up with qualified answers to them. Rather, we evolved to survive within a group of fellow humans in which simply accepting the general worldview of the group, and signalling our loyalty to that worldview (and hence to the group), was an adaptive choice most of the time. This arguably makes some sense of our tendency to accept easy answers, as well as the relative rarity of even asking such questions in the first place. Yet it obviously does not render it reasonable. If we have a question that we sincerely want answered, we should engage in critical examination and resist the ever-present temptation of accepting easy answers.

Impartiality

Impartiality refers to the principle that we should prioritize equal interests equally; that the same suffering is equally worth alleviating and preventing regardless of who experiences it. In other words, the principle of impartiality holds that it is the sentience of an individual — an individual's capacity to experience states of happiness and suffering, pleasure and pain — that makes that individual worthy of our moral concern and help, while other criteria, including an individual's gender, sexual orientation, species, and position in space and time, are not relevant per se.

Dedication to Reason

Being dedicated to reason means being willing to follow arguments and evidence, wherever these may lead us. One can argue that the principle above, impartiality, follows directly from such a dedication, because, whatever our conception of reason may be, consistency must at the very least be considered an integral part of it. And it is not consistent to treat the same thing differently — the same amount of suffering, say — depending on where in time and space it happens to be instantiated. That would be like saying that $2 + 2$ is 4 in my head, yet not necessarily in the head of any other person.[9] As utilitarian philosopher Henry Sidgwick wrote in his

---

[9] On a physicalist view of the world, this analogy could barely be closer, as we are then in both cases talking about instantiations of specific physical structures in different places, cf. Szabó, 2003.

Methods of Ethics, "Reason shows me that if my happiness is desirable and a good, the equal happiness of any other person must be equally desirable." (Book 3, Chapter 14.)

Another core virtue that follows from a dedication to reason — and which is therefore arguably not a separate core virtue, but rather a "corollary virtue"[10] — is that of cause neutrality. Cause neutrality is simply the rejection of favoritism at the level of the altruistic cause we dedicate our resources to. We should not favor, say, the alleviation of human poverty over other causes as being most important just because we happen to feel a strong attachment to it, or because we have put a lot of effort and resources into it in the past. Instead, both when it comes to different cause areas, as well as to specific interventions within these cause areas, we should remain open-minded and impartial so as to be able to follow the evidence as best we can, which leads us to the next essential virtue of effective altruism — being careful to avoid the pitfalls that prevent us from doing just that.

Being Aware of Biases

Research over the last few decades has revealed that our thinking is systematically biased in various ways.[11] Therefore, if our views and actions are to be based on reason and evidence, we must be careful to avoid these pitfalls of the human mind, the stumbling blocks to reason. I shall not review the literature on such biases here, but instead just mention a few of the most important ones we should be aware of, and which I will refer back to later in this book.

---

[10] Given a sufficiently broad conception of reason, one can, of course, argue that every reasonable claim or virtue is ultimately a corollary of (a dedication to) reason. This is indeed my own conception of reason, as outlined in Vinding, 2016d.

[11] A popular book on the subject is Daniel Kahneman's *Thinking, Fast and Slow*. Wikipedia also has an extensive list of cognitive biases: https://en.wikipedia.org/wiki/List_of_cognitive_biases

Confirmation Bias

Confirmation bias is the well-documented tendency of our minds to search for, interpret, and recall information that confirms our preexisting beliefs. [12] Not a recipe for forming reasonable beliefs, obviously. The way to counteract this bias, it would seem, is to become acutely aware of it in the first place. We can then try to counter it by suspending our attachment to our established beliefs, and by seeking out and giving fair hearing to arguments and viewpoints that may contradict our favored ones. In other words, by keeping an open mind. This is, of course, much easier said than done. Yet it is crucial, for forming good beliefs in general, and for the project of effective altruism in particular.

Overconfidence Bias

A bias closely related to confirmation bias is overconfidence bias: our tendency to have excessive confidence in our own beliefs. [13] For example, in one study, people who reported to be 100 percent certain about their answer to a question were only correct 70 to 85 percent of the time. [14] This bias should make us pause with respect to claims we profess to have 100 percent certainty in, and indeed with respect to any confidence we may have (had) in the reliability of the human mind in the first place. In the context of the pursuit of effective altruism, it should make us question even the most confident of claims we believe about which actions will help others the most. The remedy for this bias, it seems, is to compensate by weaving some humility into our credences, and by embracing intellectual humility more generally. [15]

---

[12] Plous, 1993, p. 233.

[13] Plous, 1993, pp. 219-220.

[14] Plous, 1993, pp. 219-220.

[15] It is, of course, also possible to be too humble — less certain than the evidence warrants. Yet

Wishful Thinking

Another tendency closely related to confirmation bias is our tendency to engage in wishful thinking.[16] That is, our tendency to believe what we wish were true. Recognition of this tendency should make us skeptical about those of our beliefs that happen to match up with what we wish were true — for instance, that the future will be wonderful, that life for most beings on Earth is likely to be good, or that the worst forms of suffering cannot be *that* bad. And, by extension, to pay more attention to information and arguments that suggest conclusions which are inconvenient or otherwise contrary to what we wish were true, such as the unthinkable notion that a behavior we are engaging in is wrong and should be changed, or that the world contains far more horror than we had ever imagined.

Groupthink

Groupthink refers to a phenomenon where a lack of dissenting viewpoints and critical perspectives within a group leads to irrational beliefs and decisions among its members.[17] It is the product of our general tendency to conform to our peers, not only in how we behave, but also in what we believe.[18] Continuing in the same vein as above, this should make us even more skeptical, this time toward beliefs that we happen to share with our own "group" — our peers as well as our culture at large — and cause us to practice playing the devil's advocate against these beliefs.

---

the opposite tendency, to be overconfident, does seem significantly more prevalent, and thus probably warrants more worry.

[16] Bastardi et al, 2011.

[17] Plous, 1993, pp. 203-204.

[18] Plous, 1993, pp. 203-204. More on this tendency to make our beliefs match those of our peers can be found in the book *The Elephant in the Brain* by Robin Hanson and Kevin Simler.

Scope Neglect

Also often referred to as scope insensitivity: our feelings about a disaster and our willingness to donate toward its alleviation appear largely insensitive to the number of individuals it affects.[19] This is connected to the identifiable victim effect: we generally offer greater help when we are presented with an identifiable victim of a disaster than when we are presented with facts about how many individuals it affects. And, as psychologist Paul Slovic has shown, not only does our empathy not increase as the magnitude of a disaster grows, it actually seems to decrease rapidly.[20] In terms of our immediate moral impulses, we appear more willing to help one individual than we are to help two.

This is obviously not reasonable: a disaster that involves more beings is, other things being equal, worse than one that involves fewer beings. Yet our moral sentiments somehow turn this relationship completely upside-down, which again has significant implications for any aspiring effective altruist. Most significantly, it implies that we should be skeptical of our immediate feelings about which disasters, be they ongoing or future ones, we should prioritize devoting our resources to, and that we should make an effort to consider the number of individuals involved. This may seem cold, as though we decide by considering numbers rather than individuals. Yet it is actually the opposite. For the numbers must be considered exactly because they represent individuals, individuals who would otherwise be ignored by our faulty moral intuitions. Therefore, it is to *not* consider the numbers that ultimately amounts to a failure to consider the individuals. As Michael Moor put it in his excellent TED talk "Impact through rationality", numbers count *because* individuals count.[21]

---

[19] http://www.animal-ethics.org/scope-insensitivity-failing-to-appreciate-the-numbers-of-those-who-need-our-help/

[20] Slovic, 2007.

[21] https://www.youtube.com/watch?v=PcWus1943K0

11

Speciesist Bias

The term "speciesism" refers to unjustified discrimination against beings based on their species membership.[22] And by taking seriously the ethical principle of impartiality mentioned above, we are committed to rejecting *all* forms of unjustified discrimination. In particular, we are committed to the position that, as Peter Singer puts it in the *Effective Altruism Handbook*, "[...] 'speciesism,' by analogy with racism, must also be condemned."[23]

Not surprisingly, given an evolutionary history in which killing beings of other species was necessary for human survival, and now a modern society in which we have completely trivialized the exploitation and killing of individuals of other species, this is a conclusion that we have a hard time swallowing. In other words, we humans have an enormous speciesist bias, due to biological dispositions,[24] as well as powerful cultural reinforcement of these dispositions. As a study by Lucius Caviola at the University of Oxford reported: "[...] our studies show that people morally value individuals of certain species less than others even when beliefs about intelligence and sentience are accounted for."[25] Another study

---

[22] Horta, 2010b. See also my own book on the subject, *Speciesism: Why It Is Wrong and the Implications of Rejecting It*.

[23] Carey, 2015, p. 98.

[24] Some, such as Oscar Horta, would dispute that we are at all biologically disposed to be speciesist, yet, in my view, it seems that we most likely are; that it is not merely a matter of culture that we find it difficult to include, say, octopi in our moral considerations. David Pearce argues for a view similar to mine in his anti-speciesist essay "The Anti-Speciesist Revolution", cf., for instance, the following allusion to "evolutionary reasons" for our speciesist attitudes:

> On the face of it, [the] antispeciesist claim isn't just wrong-headed; it's absurd. Philosopher Jonathan Haidt speaks of "moral dumbfounding", where we just know something is wrong but can't articulate precisely why. Haidt offers the example of consensual incest between an adult brother and sister who use birth control. For evolutionary reasons, we "just know" such an incestuous relationship is immoral. In the case of any comparisons of pigs with human infants and toddlers, we "just know" at some deep level that any alleged equivalence in status is unfounded.

[25] Caviola et al, 2018.

12

found that we are inclined to ascribe diminished mental capacities to, and even entirely deny the existence of a mind in, the non-human individuals whom we consider food. And this mind denial is increased by "expectations regarding the immediate consumption" of such beings.[26] In other words, eating a group of beings appears to make us biased with respect to the capacities we ascribe to those beings, which in turn biases our moral cognition about them.

Speciesism, as well as our speciesist bias, is something I shall go much deeper into later in this book, but suffice it for now to briefly hint at the only hopeful remedy against this bias, namely that we become extremely skeptical of our moral feelings — or perhaps rather the near-total absence thereof — and convenient rationalizations concerning the moral standing of non-human individuals.

Expected Value Thinking

The final virtue of effective altruism I shall review here is expected value thinking. Such thinking reflects the insufficiency of evaluating which possible outcomes to aim for merely in terms of the probability *or* the value of these outcomes. We have to factor both in: the estimated probability of bringing about a given outcome *multiplied by* its estimated value. This is the expected value of trying to realize this given outcome. To take a concrete example involving two betting options: say for option A we have a 50 percent probability of winning a prize of 10,000 dollars, which means that option A has an expected value of 0.5 times 10,000 dollars (= 5,000 dollars), while option B gives us a one percent chance of winning a prize of a million dollars, which yields an expected value of 0.01 times a million dollars (= 10,000 dollars). So although the probability of winning the prize is much smaller with option B, we should nonetheless

---

[26] Bastian et al, 2012.

still bet on that over option A on the expected value framework. This example illustrates that even highly unlikely outcomes can still be the most important ones to focus on according to the expected value framework, provided that they are deemed sufficiently valuable. And conversely, if the probability of winning in option B had been much lower, that even very valuable outcomes may not be the most promising to focus on, provided they are sufficiently unlikely.[27]

A specific framework often employed by effective altruists that in some sense concretizes the expected value framework is the scale, tractability, and neglectedness framework, which can help us evaluate the altruistic potential found within a given problem.

Scale, or scope, refers to the size of the problem. There is no unique measure for how to evaluate this size, but it could, for example, be in terms of how many individuals it affects, or how intense it is (e.g. intense suffering can reasonably be said to have great magnitude even if it only affects relatively few individuals). **Tractability**, sometimes called solvability, refers to how amenable to solution the problem is. That is, how much of the problem do we expect to solve per resource we spend on it? Finally, **neglectedness** is the measure of how overlooked the problem is by other people. This last consideration is relevant because a neglected problem will be more likely to have low-hanging fruits ready to be picked compared to a problem that many people are working on. Or expressed in more general terms, our efforts on more neglected problems are less likely to be subject to (as strong) diminishing returns compared to efforts on less neglected problems. Considering these three factors in combination may be helpful to get a rough sense of how much we are able to help others by spending our resources on a given problem.[28]

---

[27] For a case for why we should maximize expected value, see Brian Tomasik's essay "Why Maximize Expected Value?": http://reducing-suffering.org/why-maximize-expected-value/

[28] When we interpret these terms in a certain reasonable way, their combined product is the

Closely related to the concept of maximizing expected value is the concept of opportunity cost: the loss of potential gain from other alternatives when one alternative is chosen.[29] To choose one opportunity is to forego another, and in trying to maximize the expected value of our actions, we are essentially trying to minimize our opportunity cost by choosing the best opportunity (in expectation) that we have. Thinking in terms of opportunity cost forces us to think carefully about the alternatives to our plans, and to consider whether those alternatives might be better.

It should be noted, however, that thinking in these expected value terms is rarely, if ever, exhaustive in a good decision-making process, whether altruistic or not. We cannot always quantify the value or the probability of bringing a certain outcome about with great precision, and hence other styles of thinking will, and should, often weigh stronger in our notional decision algorithm.[30] Still, the expected value framework often has great utility, and is worth including in our considerations and decision-making process when possible.

With these principles and thinking tools in mind, let us proceed in our examination of the core question of effective altruism: how can we maximize our potential to help other individuals?

---

expected "Good done per extra person or dollar" devoted to the problem, cf. https://80000hours.org/articles/problem-framework/

[29] As defined by the *Oxford American Dictionary*. Although in economics it is defined more specifically as the value of the best option not chosen.

[30] See also Karnofsky, 2011 and Karnofsky, 2014.

MONETARY DONATION

The act of giving charitable donations is perhaps the first thing that springs to mind when it comes to actions we can take to help others in need. And it turns out that such donations actually can go a surprisingly long way. Let us review some estimates of just how far they can go in different spheres.

Human Poverty

The organization GiveWell evaluates charities that help humans in the developing world in order to find out which of them achieve the most per dollar donated. GiveWell cites two reasons for this focus on people in the developing world: 1) poor people in richer countries are "wealthy by developing-world standards", and 2) probably for this first reason, GiveWell has found no poverty-targeting interventions in richer countries that compare favorably to its most recommended interventions in the developing world.[31]

One of the charities that GiveWell recommends most highly is the Against Malaria Foundation (AMF), a charity that enables the distribution of cheap bed nets that have been shown to reduce child mortality and malaria cases in developing countries. On GiveWell's estimates, a human

---

[31] https://www.givewell.org/how-we-work/process#GlobalPoor

death from malaria is prevented for roughly every 3,300 US dollars donated to AMF.[32] Other charities recommended as highly effective by GiveWell at the time of writing include the Schistosomiasis Control Initiative, which treats people for extremely painful parasite infections in sub-Saharan Africa; Evidence Action's Deworm the World Initiative, also treating parasitic infections; and the Helen Keller International vitamin A supplementation program, doing what the name suggests, providing vitamin A supplementation, which is a cheap way to reduce child mortality.

In a world where more than five million children under the age of five die every year, and where more than half of these deaths "are due to conditions that could be prevented or treated with access to simple, affordable interventions",[33] it is difficult to defend not doing *something*.[34] And upon deciding to do something, it seems difficult to defend not examining how we can do the *best* something. It would be tragic to fail to save a life — and hence, in a sense, kill a person, albeit by omission[35] — by spending one's altruistically devoted resources in a suboptimal way. The imperative of avoiding such tragically suboptimal actions is, of course, not particular to the cause of human poverty, but applies to the

---

[32] https://www.givewell.org/how-we-work/our-criteria/cost-effectiveness/cost-effectiveness-models

[33] http://www.who.int/mediacentre/factsheets/fs178/en/

[34] As demonstrated well by Singer's shallow pond argument, and as argued at greater length in Peter Unger's *Living High & Letting Die: Our Illusion of Innocence.*

[35] Although there is something to be said in favor of the difference in how our moral intuitions evaluate acts of omission and acts of commission respectively, I think we are generally overstating the difference. Together with Singer's shallow pond argument, I find the following resources valuable for helping us question our, in my view, flawed view of the ethical status of acts of omission:
https://www.youtube.com/watch?v=PcWus1943K0 ("Impact through rationality: Michael Moor")
https://www.youtube.com/watch?v=-4rh5L4iluw ("Our daily life and death decisions: Adriano Mannino")

endeavor of effective altruism altogether. Avoiding this mistake is essentially what effective altruism is all about.

Meta Charity

Raising for Effective Giving (REG) is a meta charity in that it raises money for other effective charities. It does this by appealing mostly to professional poker players, people who are used to thinking in terms of maximizing expected value, and who may therefore be inclined to let their altruistic impulse be translated into a donation expected to have a high value. And from professional poker players, a donation of even a small percentage of a winning prize is still a lot of money.

The charities that receive the money REG raises include the organizations mentioned above, as well as others that REG believes help sentient beings cost-effectively. So why would one want to donate one's money to REG rather than just donating directly to those charities? One reason is that REG moves 16 dollars to its recommended charities for every dollar it spends on fundraising work.[36] Thus, supporting REG's fundraising work may end up resulting in a significantly higher donation to a top-rated charity than would a direct donation.

Whether this is the best decision to make depends on other considerations as well, however, such as whether a single dollar donated directly to one of REG's top charities today might be more valuable than 16 dollars later down the line, as well as how much room for funding REG has with respect to its fundraising projects. So the choice to go all meta donation is not necessarily an obvious one, although it certainly is appealing.

Such fund-multiplying charity is not the only form of meta charity. Other meta charities include the organizations that evaluate charities, such

---

[36] https://reg-charity.org/about/transparency/

as GiveWell mentioned above, as well as the organization Giving What We Can (GWWC), which also focuses on helping people in the developing world. By donating to such charities rather than to the charities they recommend, one should expect to improve the quality of their recommendations, however marginally. Whether this will be the optimal decision depends on how much better one expects these evaluators' recommendations to be as a result of the added resources, which should then be compared to what the evaluatees could do with the resources — and also on whether the evaluator and evaluatee indeed focus on the most promising cause in the first place, e.g. global poverty as opposed to, say, helping non-human animals.

An organization that does charity evaluation within the latter cause — advocating for the interests of non-human individuals and sparing them from unnecessary suffering and death — is Animal Charity Evaluators (ACE), whose recommendations we shall take a closer look at now.

Helping Non-Human Individuals

The vast majority of sentient beings on the planet, more than 99.99 percent of them, are non-human.[37] In spite of this, virtually none of humanity's charitable donations are devoted to this group of beings. These two facts alone strongly suggest that we can help non-human individuals a lot with our limited resources, a suggestion emphatically borne out by more elaborate estimates.

The best estimates from ACE suggest that one can expect a donation of 1,000 US dollars to the best charities within this cause to spare more than 4,000 beings from a life on a factory farm.[38] This is an enormous number, so large that we, in order to get a sense of its moral magnitude,

---

[37] https://reg-charity.org/about/transparency/ For some concrete estimates, see http://reducing-suffering.org/how-many-wild-animals-are-there/

[38] https://animalcharityevaluators.org/donation-advice/donation-impact/

probably need to remind ourselves of our scope neglect — our inability to appreciate the difference between helping 1, 10, 100, 1,000, and 4,000 individuals. More than that, we should also expect our moral intuitions to fail to appreciate the value of helping so many such beings due to our speciesist bias.

The top charities that ACE recommends within this cause are, at the moment of writing, The Humane League, Animal Equality, and The Good Food Institute. Another charity that deserves mention, and which ACE has recommended as a standout charity in the past, is Animal Ethics. This charity is unique in that it focuses on advocating for *all* non-human individuals, including those living in nature, which turn out to be the vast majority of non-human individuals.[39] In my view, almost all other charities within this cause have an enormous bias toward neglecting this vast majority — a neglect that cannot be defended.[40]

To make the blasphemous, yet for effective altruism essential, move of comparing causes, specifically the best estimates of the best donation opportunities within two of the causes we have visited so far, we get that for the 3,300 US dollars we can save a human life with by donating to AMF, we can save more than 13,000 non-human individuals from a life on a factory farm. I shall not discuss the value of these alternatives here, but merely let it suffice to note, for now at least, that it is far from clear that

---

[39] Again, for some concrete estimates, see http://reducing-suffering.org/how-many-wild-animals-are-there/

[40] Although a disproportionate focus on beings exploited by humans may make sense, a near-total neglect of the rest can by no means be justified. For more on this point, see the following essay: https://sentience-politics.org/animal-advocates-focus-antispeciesism-not-veganism/ as well as my book *Speciesism: Why It Is Wrong and the Implications of Rejecting It*. As far as I can tell, the estimates from ACE themselves are also polluted by such a bias, as they generally don't seem to factor in the impact that an intervention may have on non-human individuals in nature (for some ideas on why we largely ignore wild animals in our moral considerations, see http://reducing-suffering.org/why-most-people-dont-care-about-wild-animal-suffering/). Given that these beings comprise the vast majority of non-human beings — and hence the vast majority of all sentient beings on the planet — this cannot be defended.

the alleviation of human poverty is the best thing we can spend our limited resources on. Indeed, the claim that it is should be met with skepticism in light of the above.

Effective Altruism Research

Another potentially promising donation opportunity is that of funding research into effective altruism — research into how we can best help others. The work done by the charity evaluators mentioned above can, of course, be counted as examples of such research, and their findings reveal the enormous value of supporting research into effective altruism. Without it, we would not have qualified estimates about which charities of the kind mentioned above are most worth supporting.

Yet there are forms of research that go much deeper. For the charity evaluators mentioned above — GiveWell, GWWC, and ACE — can hardly be claimed to actively do research from a starting point of cause neutrality, as they all focus on a particular cause that they have chosen to settle on. Their choices may reflect a cause-neutral analysis of what cause is most sensible to focus on, yet making such analyses is not itself the focus of these organizations. It is that of other organizations, however, such as the Foundational Research Institute (FRI), which states its mission in the following way:

> Our mission is to identify cooperative and effective strategies to reduce involuntary suffering. We believe that in a complex world where the long-run consequences of our actions are highly uncertain, such an undertaking requires foundational research. Currently, our research focuses on reducing risks of dystopian futures in the context of emerging technologies.[41]

---

[41] https://foundational-research.org/

21

This is a different, more open-ended approach than that of the charity evaluators previously mentioned, and as the quote hints, through such foundational (cause-neutral) research, FRI has landed on the provisional focus that is risks of bad outcomes due to emerging technology, particularly artificial intelligence.[42] And FRI is not alone in this. Other organizations with a strong focus on artificial intelligence, and which can also be considered part of the effective altruism movement, include the Future of Humanity Institute (FHI) at the University of Oxford and the Machine Intelligence Research Institute (MIRI). FHI does research into other areas as well, and is arguably also cause-neutral,[43] while MIRI is more narrowly focused on artificial intelligence. I shall postpone the explanation of this focus on artificial intelligence until the following chapter. For now, I will just note that it very much remains an open question whether such a focus really is what a complete, cause-neutral analysis would recommend.

Another organization that does research of a more general nature than charity evaluation, and whose mission comprises a possible rival candidate as the most promising cause to focus on, is Sentience Institute (SI). Its goal is simple: to expand humanity's moral circle.[44] This goal is, of course, highly complementary to the work of ACE and its recommended charities, yet it is still different in that 1) SI's research takes a more general approach to how we can best expand humanity's moral circle, and 2) this research appears to pertain more directly to all sentient beings in the

---

[42] https://foundational-research.org/altruists-should-prioritize-artificial-intelligence/

[43] "Arguably", because it is arguably biased toward focusing on the reduction of the probability of human extinction without taking (sufficiently) seriously the possibility of scenarios in which human extinction would be preferable (on various axiological views). We may be tempted to say "Oh, that's a very low probability", but our well-documented tendency to entertain wishful thinking alone should make us skeptical of this convenient belief.

[44] https://www.sentienceinstitute.org/

future, including non-biological beings. Whether this more general approach will be better than more direct efforts is highly uncertain, however.

It is no doubt difficult to put numbers on the value of such research into effective altruism. There is no easy way to make a controlled experiment that assesses whether the work of the kind that FRI and SI do is cost-effective or not. The general and reflective nature of such research inevitably makes evaluations of its value more difficult — compared to, say, zooming in on an intervention and asking what its immediate effects are. Yet this very generality — the consideration of a wider array of possible focus areas and the study of more diverse sources of knowledge — is exactly what makes such research promising. Not many people are doing such work, and if crucial considerations that force our altruistic priorities to change altogether emerge as the result of it, such work could well turn out to be unsurpassably important.

Which donation opportunities are best with respect to the goal of helping sentient individuals as much as possible is a question we will probably never be able to answer with great confidence. Yet to the extent that we can answer it with at least some confidence, such an answer is going to depend upon deeper considerations than any we have raised so far, such as what helping others means more precisely. These are considerations we shall delve into in later chapters.

CAREER CHOICE

How much we are able to help other individuals will in large part be determined by what career we choose. In one way, this is rather obvious: a significant part of our waking lives will be spent doing professional work, which renders our choice of career a most important one with respect to our potential to help others.

The organization 80,000 Hours, whose name derives from the number of hours the average person can expect to spend on their career, was founded precisely with the purpose of helping people find the career with the greatest altruistic potential. What such a career might be for any given individual is, of course, a difficult question, and again one we will likely never have definitive answers to. Yet this does not imply that we cannot come up with highly qualified principles and guesses that are worth following to maximize the altruistic impact of our careers.

One such principle, or rather counter-principle, that 80,000 Hours emphasizes is "don't follow your passion". This may seem counter-intuitive, and not least contrary to everything found in the modern canon of popular motivational speeches. Yet it is not entirely so. For the point is not that one should not be highly passionate about what one does — that is indeed recommendable, probably even necessary. Rather, the point is that our passions can change over time, and the thing we are most passionate about at the moment 1) might not be what we will be most passionate about in the future, and 2) might not be something that there is a demand for, or which otherwise helps other individuals much.

So instead of indulging in our immediate passions, 80,000 Hours recommends that we make a careful analysis of which career paths seem to have the best altruistic impact, and to then consider pursuing the optimal path. And here one should, of course, remember that different individuals have different talents and dispositions that to a great extent determine what careers they can be successful in.

A related consideration is how fulfilling one would find a given career path. This is relevant for many reasons: it can be difficult to be altruistically motivated if one is unfulfilled; an unfulfilling career path is less sustainable than a fulfilling one (and thus the risk of burnout is higher); and we are generally also more productive in our work the happier we are.[45]

Also relevant are the counterfactuals: what would happen if you did not take a given career path? Would someone else take it, and if so, would they have a better or worse altruistic impact through it than you? If they would have a better impact, or even an equally good one, it might be better for you to choose another path where you would make a greater difference, all things considered.[46]

So upon engaging in such a deeper analysis, we see that the question is not just, "What job that helps others a lot could I do well?", but also, "What job that helps others a lot could I do *particularly* well?" and "What difference can I make that would not have happened otherwise?" In this way, the analysis quickly becomes rather complex, dependent not just

---

[45] Tenney et al, 2016.

[46] And this may also hold true even if they had a significantly worse impact than you, cf. the concept of comparative advantage.

upon the countless opportunities and talents we have ourselves, but also on the opportunities, talents, and choices of other people.

In terms of more general career advice, 80,000 Hours recommends viewing one's career plan as a best guess in progress, a hypothesis that one tests and updates continuously to get a better sense of one's own personal fit to a given career path, including how much of a difference one could make in it. They also recommend that one focuses on learning a set of skills that can be useful later — to build a large so-called career capital.

Earning to Give

An idea often associated with effective altruism is that of pursuing a high-earning career in order to donate a lot of money to charity, commonly referred to as Earning to Give. In concrete terms, this could mean becoming a trader at a hedge fund, or starting a start-up.[47]

At the first level of analysis of the counterfactuals, this seems a promising path. An altruistic person taking a job at a hedge fund to donate a large fraction of the high salary likely has high value compared to someone else taking that same job, as that someone else likely would not donate nearly as much, if anything. In this way, a person who pursues such a path may be able to fund the salary of several people working at a non-profit organization. Compare this to the counterfactual value of person A choosing to take a job in a non-profit that would otherwise have been taken by person B. The difference between the work that person A and person B could do would have to be huge in order for it to be bigger than the difference that could be made by several additional employees funded by a high-earning person doing Earning to Give.[48]

---

[47] See for instance the following essays:

https://80000hours.org/2017/05/how-much-do-hedge-fund-traders-earn/
https://80000hours.org/career-reviews/tech-entrepreneurship/

[48] It should be noted, of course, that few people will be able to successfully pursue a high-

So Earning to Give appears to be a promising path. Yet there are also counter-considerations suggesting that it might not be ideal, at least for many people. One is that of personal fit: taking a lucrative career may afford a high altruistic impact, yet most people cannot earn a high salary, and even if one could get a high-earning job, working such a job may not be suitable for various reasons.[49]

Another consideration against Earning to Give is that many non-profit organizations, including most of the major ones that identify as being part of the effective altruism movement, report being significantly more constrained by talent than by funding, meaning that getting more competent people to work for them is a greater bottleneck for the progress of their work than a lack of money is.[50] This is not to say that Earning to Give is not important, or even that it is not neglected by aspiring altruists, but rather that there are other things that appear even more neglected.[51] For example, in one survey, the three most wanted skills at prominent organizations in the effective altruism movement were, in order of importance, 1) Good calibration, wide knowledge and ability to work out what is important, 2) Generalist research, and 3) Managing.[52]

In other words, with the competence of being widely read and clear-thinking listed as both number one and two, it seems that undertaking the

---

earning career, and if we select such a rare case with respect to Earning to Give, we should, to be fair, also do so in the case of our notional person A, i.e. assume that person A is exceptionally skilled at the work in question, in which case it is not that unthinkable that the difference between person A and B really could be bigger than the difference made by several additional employees.

[49] See for instance the following personal account: https://80000hours.org/2015/06/why-i-stopped-earning-to-give/

[50] https://80000hours.org/2017/11/talent-gaps-survey-2017

[51] https://80000hours.org/2015/11/why-you-should-focus-more-on-talent-gaps-not-funding-gaps/

[52] https://80000hours.org/2017/11/talent-gaps-survey-2017/

classical virtues of reading widely and thinking deeply about what is most important, and doing so full-time if possible, might actually be even more important than Earning to Give, especially if one is well-suited for such things. And it can, of course, be reasonably argued that one should practice such virtues regardless of time commitment.

The above has just been a shallow overview of the advice provided by 80,000 Hours. Fortunately, as an organization devoted to effective altruism, 80,000 Hours provides its resources free on their website, 80000hours.org. Additionally, they have a book on the subject: *80,000 Hours: Find a fulfilling career that does good*, by 80,000 Hours co-founder Benjamin Todd.

In sum, our choice of career is a consequential one for our future altruistic potential, and which career is best depends on many things, including our own talents and dispositions, as well as what other people are and could be doing. It also depends on the deeper considerations alluded to at the end of the previous chapter concerning questions of a more fundamental nature. Questions we shall turn to soon.

THE LONG-TERM FUTURE

Taking seriously the core effective altruist principle of impartiality implies that we must include *all* sentient beings[53] in our moral considerations, regardless not only of their race, sexuality, and species, but also where in time and space they find themselves. In particular, it implies that we must take the moral value of future individuals seriously, especially since the number of beings who will exist tomorrow, and in the following tomorrows, will likely be much greater than the number of beings alive today.

Expressed less metaphorically, we can expect that the vast majority of sentient beings whom our actions can affect will exist beyond the next couple of decades — the couple of decades that are the prime focus of most contemporary political and ethical debates. This has profound implications for the project of effective altruism, and forces us to consider everything we have seen so far in a new light. It suggests that the main criterion for evaluating how much a given action helps other individuals may be its expected impact on the long-term future.[54]

---

[53] At least all beings whom we can impact in some way.

[54] The following essay argues for a similar conclusion: https://ea-foundation.org/blog/the-importance-of-the-far-future/

If we consider the long-term future as a cause to focus on in light of the aforementioned scope, tractability, and neglectedness framework, we see that it does superlatively well on two of these criteria, while its status is somewhat uncertain on the third one. First, there is its scope, which could barely be greater: we should expect the vast majority of sentient beings whom our actions can impact to exist beyond the next couple of decades that usually steal most of our altruistic attention. And this short altruistic attention span then leads us to the neglectedness of the long-term future, which could not be much greater either, for various reasons.

First, as creatures who evolved to focus on our survival moment-to-moment, and for whom it was generally costly to move any attention away from the near future, it is not surprising that we pay less attention to the far future than deeper philosophical reflection suggests we should. Second, beyond our evolved nature, we also live in a social world that does not strongly incentivize us to make an effort to positively impact the future beyond the next few decades. Politicians are incentivized to focus mostly on the next couple of elections, companies must focus on making profits on a year-by-year basis and virtually never plan more than a couple of decades ahead, and the same generally applies to the focus of non-profits, which are under pressure to demonstrate immediate tangible results.

Thus, both the scope and the neglectedness of the long-term future is clearly enormous, and how such a neglect can exist in spite of the enormous scope seems explainable, at least in part, by naturally emerged limitations of our minds and social structures. Yet it may also have something to do with the final, as yet unvisited criterion: the tractability of improving the long-term future. For it may just be really difficult to impact the long-term future in a positive way, and in the absence of any concrete suggestions about how we might improve the far future, it should perhaps not be surprising that we are not acting on such suggestions. Yet whether said tractability is really that low remains an open question.

Relatively little attention has been devoted to the question, which suggests that more research should be a high priority, as there may be low-hanging fruit that can readily be picked. Qualified ideas for improving the long-term future might then make such long-term improvement less neglected, as it may give people more concrete suggestions to act upon.

All in all, a strong case can be made that we should devote much more attention to the long-term future, especially in the form of research on how we can best help its inhabitants.

Future Egalitarianism

Most contemporary discussions about how we can prioritize and distribute resources in a just and ethical way seem to take place within a framework where we look at the world, which sadly only means humanity, in its present state, and then try to work out how we can spend or distribute resources in a way that is optimal for these individuals.

Yet if we take impartiality seriously, this framework, while no doubt reasonable and useful in some contexts, is clearly lacking, as it fails to take far future individuals into consideration (not to mention the vast majority of sentient beings alive today: non-human individuals). If we correct for this failure and consider the entire mass of sentient beings whom our actions can impact, we realize that the most neglected group of beings, in terms of where we devote our resources today, are probably found in the long-term future.[55] To put it somewhat provocatively, in terms of how we spend our current resources, all humans alive today probably belong to "the one percent", and most likely far less, compared to the beings of the far future, suggesting that if we want to direct our resources

---

[55] One may object that the future will be better able to care for itself than we are, in part

because it will be so much wealthier than we are today. Yet while this may well be true for powerful agents of the far future, it is far from clear that it holds true for vulnerable far future beings. I will say a bit more on this matter in the section "Expanding Our Moral Circle" found in the penultimate chapter.

— be it in terms of donations, volunteer time, or indeed our entire career — to a group of neglected beings, we should direct them in ways that will help these far future beings.[56]

So how do we best help beings in the far future, then? Could it not be by helping beings alive today? Perhaps it could.

Long-Term Impact: Direct or Indirect Action?

A useful distinction in this context is that between direct and indirect ways of impacting the far future. A direct way could be to work on a specific technology or social institution that one expects to exist and be influential in the long-term future, while indirect ways include more general actions such as advocating on behalf of the individuals who are worst off today, or educating people about important things, which may then — in a more indirect, ripple effect manner — lead to a better long-term future. Effects of this latter kind have been referred to as long-run indirect effects, or flow-through effects.[57]

Whether the best way to impact the far future is via direct or indirect efforts is very much an open question. An argument in favor of focusing on indirect ways is that the values of future individuals are extremely important, and maybe the best way to positively impact these values — to increase future concern for the beings who are worst off, say — is to push for concrete interventions that promote such values in the here-and-now. In this way, it could be that supporting the charities mentioned in the previous chapter focused on relatively short-term betterment, such as AMF or ACE, may also be optimal with respect to the long-term future.

---

[56] In this way, one can argue that many versions of prioritarianism, as well as egalitarianism, would imply that we should focus predominantly on the far future.

[57] This distinction between direct and indirect ways of impacting the future is, of course, far from clear-cut. Many projects and interventions can reasonably be identified as both.

One can, of course, reasonably argue that we should be skeptical of such a convenient convergence between short-term and long-term optimal courses of action. Yet one can also reasonably be skeptical of the merits of such skepticism. After all, why should what looks optimal from a short-term perspective not be optimal with respect to the long-term too? For example, it seems plausible that a person in the year 1800 who wanted to minimize future racism would have the most success by working on the concrete, *near-term* goal of abolishing race-based slavery. Yet it is, of course, far from obvious, as is generally true of assessments of far future interventions.

Regardless of whether we think short-term and long-term optimal interventions happen to converge, it is important to avoid the non sequitur that the importance of the long-term future implies that *only* the long-term future matters. That simply does not follow. "It's just near-term suffering, so it doesn't matter that much in the great scheme of things" is not a notion we entertain when it comes to our own suffering, and neither should we when it comes to the suffering of our contemporaries.

The Future of Artificial Intelligence

Working to positively impact the future of artificial intelligence is an example of a direct effort to improve the long-term future.[58] The reasons behind this focus are presented most elaborately in the book *Superintelligence: Paths, Dangers, Strategies* by philosopher Nick Bostrom, but the short version goes roughly as follows: The main reason that humans rule the Earth is our intelligence, which in this context means our cognitive abilities, and so as we create more cognitively capable systems that pursue their pre-programmed goals more intelligently than humans can, there is a risk that such systems will assume control of the

---

[58] https://foundational-research.org/altruists-should-prioritize-artificial-intelligence/
https://intelligence.org/why-ai-safety/

world based on these pre-programmed goals. Therefore, the argument goes, we better make sure we get these goals and their implementation right so as to avoid bad outcomes, an effort that has become known as AI safety. This is in large part the reason organizations like FRI, FHI, and MIRI focus heavily on artificial intelligence.

Whether AI safety is indeed the best way to create a better future has also been disputed by some effective altruists, however.[59] Economist and FHI research associate Robin Hanson, for instance, has argued that it is highly unlikely that the future will depend crucially on how a single, or even a few, powerful software programs are designed.[60] The argument by Hanson and others is not that AI safety is unimportant, but rather that there are other problems that appear even more urgent. In other words, they are arguing that we should carefully consider the opportunity cost of AI safety work, and give consideration to other top candidates before we grant it the title of "most promising endeavor", which seems difficult to argue with. After all, the scenario in which one or more software programs abruptly take over the world is but one among many possible future scenarios, and it seems reasonable to distribute our long-term future focus and preparation to a broader class of outcomes than just this one.

So while impacting the future of artificial intelligence is considered a promising way to positively influence the future by many effective altruists, there is still much room for disagreement about what kind of work has the *greatest* expected value. For instance, even if the future of artificial intelligence is all-important, this does not imply that we should necessarily focus mostly on software design in order to "design" the best future, as opposed to, say, the larger system in which the software will be integrated, e.g. at the level of social, political, or corporate structures. At

---

[59] See for instance the following reading list (not all authors identify as effective altruists): https://magnusvinding.com/2017/12/16/a-contra-ai-foom-reading-list/

[60] See for instance http://www.overcomingbias.com/2014/07/30855.html

the very least, it seems reasonable not to be too quick to accept premature answers in either direction on this issue — e.g. "AI safety is clearly the most important cause" or "AI safety is clearly *not* the most important cause" — and to avoid being too quick to ignore other causes and ways to impact the long-term future when we know so little.

In concluding this chapter, it is worth noting that there are some significant caveats to focusing on the long-term future. One such caveat is that the long-term future of our civilization is less certain to exist than the short-term future is, and if the probability of imminent extinction is sufficiently high, it makes little sense to focus on the long-term future. It is, however, difficult to say what a plausible estimate of this probability might be, and the possibility that the future of our civilization will last millions of years can by no means be ruled out. Therefore, one can reasonably argue that, in light of the uncertainty of how likely extinction is, we should still focus the most on longer-term outcomes, as they contain more value (cf. the expected value framework).[61] Nonetheless, this consideration does arguably have the implication that we should update somewhat toward strategies that are also positive from a short-term perspective. In other words, that we to a greater extent should seek to pursue actions that seem "timescale robust" — robust across *both* the short and long term.

Another caveat is that the long-term future seems more difficult to reliably influence than the near-term future, and it seems more difficult the longer the term gets. This, of course, does not render the long-term future unimportant. It still seems that more research into the question of how to

---

[61] This consideration about extinction probability does, however, dampen what a more immediate and naive analysis of the importance of the far future would suggest. In relation to the question concerning short versus long-term future focus, see also the following essays: http://reducing-suffering.org/altruists-focus-reducing-short-term-far-future-suffering/ http://prioritizationresearch.com/should-altruists-prioritize-the-far-future/

best impact the long-term future should be among our highest priorities. Yet we should be realistic about what to expect: highly uncertain answers, at best of a modestly qualified kind.

So although the impact our actions have on the long-term future does seem the most important thing about them, it is far from clear how to make this impact the best we can. And, much more fundamentally, before we can begin to say what is best in the long-term, or the short-term for that matter, we must have greater clarity about what "best" even means, which is what we shall turn to now.

THE CRUCIALITY OF
CLARITY ABOUT VALUES

What we have seen so far in our examination of how to best help others has been of a rather general nature, in two senses. First, it is general in that the ideas and considerations we have visited are ones that people in the effective altruism movement tend mostly to agree with. Second, it is general in that we have phrased our project in rather generic terms: how can we best help, or benefit, others? We have said nothing about what benefiting or helping others in fact means in more specific terms, nor about what constitutes the greatest such help. In other words, we have been thoroughly imprecise and unreflective. And while this was perhaps permissible for the purpose of presenting the preceding considerations, it will not do for any serious project of effective altruism. For how can we systematically try to help or improve the world as much as possible if we do not have decent clarity about what this means? In order to prioritize and navigate meaningfully and effectively toward the goal of helping others, we must have greater clarity about what this goal entails.

One might say that specifying the meaning of "helping others" beyond our shared common sense understanding of it amounts to little more than philosophical hair-splitting. After all, don't we know what helping and benefiting others is when we see it? Yet this sentiment, while intuitive and understandable, is misguided. The problem is that when it comes to helping or benefiting others, common sense is a lot less common than one might be inclined to think. For instance, on the subject of population ethics, we find widely held views that are, at least in some sense, diametrically opposed. On the one hand, there are philosophers who believe that we should bring about as much well-being as possible (the greatest amount of happiness minus suffering, roughly speaking), while on the other, there are many philosophers who defend a view referred to as the Asymmetry, which holds that "while it detracts from the value of an outcome to add individuals whose lives are of overall negative value, it does not increase the value of an outcome to add individuals whose lives are of overall positive value."[62] Given such a disagreement, it is unclear what could meaningfully be considered "common sense" when it comes to helping others. And that is just considering disagreements about population ethics.

On the simplest of matters, we of course do agree. Bringing water to the thirsty clearly constitutes help, and the same can be said about curing a person of a painful disease. But beyond these simplest of matters, the meaning of "helping others" really is quite poorly specified, and plausible arguments and intuitions often point in quite different, even inconsistent, directions. So, to reiterate, any attempt to systematically help others based merely on "the" common sense definition of this term *is* an ill-defined endeavor. The pursuit of effective altruism in the absence of careful specification of what benefiting others means is bound to be ineffective.

This is less clear when we focus only on the short-term, where we can at least readily identify actions that clearly constitute *a* help to other beings by common sense and consensus (though probably not what would constitute *the greatest* help), but as we extend our focus to the farther future, the need for greater clarity and precision becomes increasingly

---

[62] Holtug, 2004.

clear. Considering the aforementioned divergence on population ethics, for instance, it is unclear whether we should aim to drastically increase the number of sentient beings in the universe to maximize the total amount of well-being, or whether we should not consider this a priority at all. Thus, even when comparing two widely held views on values, we readily find enormous differences in terms of their practical implications — a future full of sentient life versus an empty one, say — which highlights the cruciality of reflecting deeply on our values.

Helping Others: "What" and "How"

A distinction that illustrates the point made above, as well as where we tend to go wrong, is that between 1) *what* helping or benefiting others amounts to, and 2) *how* that is best achieved. These are two very different questions, and answering the second one in a qualified manner requires us to have a qualified answer to the first one. And where we go wrong is that we focus almost solely on the second question, "*How* can we improve the world?", rather than first asking, "*What* is the end goal of world improvement?" We are eager to act rather than reflect, which is understandable, yet unrigorous, and ultimately leaves us without a well-defined goal we can meaningfully pursue.

This distinction also hints at a parallel distinction between two different kinds of unclarity, namely a lack of clarity about 1) and 2) above. The first one may be called value unclarity — i.e. a lack of clarity about what kind of help, or more generally what state of affairs, that is of the greatest value — while the second one may be called empirical uncertainty, and is the lack of clarity we have regarding how to best achieve the "what".[63] Uncertainty of the latter kind seems widely acknowledged and talked about, and is also the kind of uncertainty that we

[63] Phrased in somewhat broader terms, we may also define empirical uncertainty as uncertainty about what the actual state of the world is and how to achieve an (already specified) ideal one.

have been referring to in previous chapters, while a lack of clarity of the former kind seems talked about a lot less. For instance, in the effective altruism community, people commonly acknowledge that there is great uncertainty about what specific action is "most effective", where this uncertainty appears to only refer to empirical uncertainty. That is, it seems tacitly assumed that there is some underlying, well-defined view of values, or end goals, that is shared by everyone. Yet again, this is rarely the case.

Inescapable Unclarity

Empirical uncertainty is inescapable. There is much we do not know, and cannot know, about the current state of the world, and the question of how we can make the future unfold in accordance with some specific goal is bound to be even more uncertain still, as it implies knowledge about not just one, but countless world states over time, as well as knowledge about how such states change as a consequence of various hypothetical actions. To represent the unfolding of the future requires much information, and anything beyond highly coarse-grained models of alternative such unfoldings — or even a single one — is simply impossible to create due to the limited information available to us in the present. Expressed simply: we can never know the exact consequences of our actions.[64]

But what about value unclarity, then? May we not be able to reduce this down to nil? Almost surely not, and for a similar reason: we cannot specify the value of the many possible states that the world can assume, or indeed even its actual states. Consider a system like a live human brain, for example. The number of possible brain states is just too vast for us to be able to determine, or indeed even contemplate, what value we would assign each of them.[65] And so too with the actual states of, say, all animal

---

[64] For some considerations of the implications of this fact, see for instance https://foundational-research.org/charity-cost-effectiveness-in-an-uncertain-world/

[65] This is not to say that the states of a system like, say, a biological brain are necessarily all

brains on our planet in the present moment. Even in that case the number of states is too great, and the respective states too complex, for us to make qualified estimates, indeed just any estimate, of the value of each state individually. All we can do is to make very rough and generalizing assessments of their value.[66]

This leaves us in quite a predicament: not only can we not say how to best achieve some precisely specified goal, but we cannot even specify such a goal in the first place. In both instances, we are forced to speak in highly coarse-grained terms. So what does this mean for the call for greater clarity about our values? Apart from giving us an important sense of realism about what such clarity will look like in the best case, namely much less than perfectly detailed, it does not change much. We can still gain far more clarity about values, about the "what", than what we have today, and greater such clarity remains crucial. A rough blueprint is still much better than nothing, and the more detailed it is, the better.

Clarifying the "What"

So where do we start in order to gain clarity about this matter of value? An obvious place to start might be to consider different theories about what things are valuable and/or normative. Three prominent classes of such theories are virtue ethics (roughly: we should be virtuous), deontological

---

that matter — that states of such systems comprise an exhaustive account of the "what" question. Yet on any plausible view of what has value/what helping others means, this is at least a subset of what is valuable and/or should count (i.e. on any plausible value system, one must, at the very least, clarify which brains are sentient). And additional value entities or criteria only render specification of the "what" even more complicated.

[66] Alternatively, think of it in terms of ideal world states: we cannot even specify what state of

the world would be ideal in just a single instant — in terms of precise physical specification, that is — much less over the course of the entire future of our civilization. At most, all we can specify are highly compressed and coarse-grained models of what states of the world we consider ideal. One can thus think of altruism in terms of a matching effort: trying to make the actual state of the world match some ideal state of the world, but where our information about both, i.e. the actual state and the ideal state, is bound to be extremely limited. *Effective* altruism, then, is the project of navigating this predicament wisely.

ethics (roughly: we should act according to certain duties), and consequentialist ethics. Most self-identified effective altruists lean toward the latter view, consequentialism, according to which it is the consequences of our actions that determine their value and normativity. Yet even if we were to declare ourselves full-blooded consequentialists, we would still have a long way to go toward specifying our values, as we would then still need to clarify what *kinds* of consequences, or states of the world, that are of greater value than others. We may do this by saying that we are consequentialists of the utilitarian flavor,[67] yet this is just a small step toward further specification, as there are also many different kinds of utilitarianism, and they can differ quite radically from each other in what they hold to be valuable, and hence also in terms of their practical implications. In the standard formulation,[68] utilitarianism holds that we should bring about the greatest sum of happiness minus suffering, commonly referred to as hedonistic utilitarianism. Another version, preference utilitarianism, holds that we should maximize not happiness, but preference satisfaction minus preference frustration. And even quite similar versions of these two theories can have radically different implications. Beyond that, there are also negative versions of both these kinds of utilitarianism, which give priority to the minimization of suffering and preference frustration respectively, and the difference in practical implications between negative and non-negative versions of the same theory can be quite extreme.

Now, it may be tempting to think that if we specify our view down to the level of granularity we have zoomed in on at this point, then we would be close to having a sufficiently specific view of what has value. Yet this is far from the case. For even if we decide to subscribe to, say, a version of

---

[67] Oscar Horta urged me to here mention that there are prominent consequentialist theories that are not utilitarian, such as egalitarianism and prioritarianism.

[68] And in Jeremy Bentham's original formulation of (his version of) the theory.

negative hedonistic utilitarianism — i.e. we prioritize reducing conscious experiences of suffering — we will still be left with many open questions. For example, what kind of priority do we give suffering? Is the reduction of suffering *all* that matters? And how do we prioritize different kinds of suffering? For instance, should we give greater priority to extreme suffering than to mild forms of suffering, perhaps so much so that it is impossible for any number of mildly bad experiences to be worse than a single very bad one? These are all crucial questions that we must consider in order to be clear about what we are aiming for. And then we haven't even yet raised the question of what suffering itself is in more precise terms.

Specifying the Nature of the (Under)Specified "What"

In one sense, we all know what words like "happiness" and "suffering" mean. In another sense, however, we are deeply ignorant. A useful analogy might be an 18th century understanding of disease: people back then perhaps knew a disease like leprosy when they saw it, yet they had no understanding of the underlying mechanics. They did not have knowledge of bacterial and viral infections, nor of genetic disorders. And this is roughly how well we understand happiness and suffering today — we can recognize and point to some cases of it, but a more detailed understanding escapes us.

We of course do know that happiness and suffering are somehow mediated by states of the brain, yet this is not very specific, and also does not tell us much about what other systems mediate such states. It is about as detailed and useful as the 18th century person's knowledge that disease has something to do with the state of the body. Such a person would not be fit to be a doctor. Nor are we, without a decent description and understanding of what suffering is in physical terms, well fit to act toward its minimization.

43

This conclusion applies not only to the reduction of suffering, but to any effort to act in accordance with the principle of impartiality, as any such effort requires us to know what the physical signatures of sentience are. Are insects sentient? What about computer simulations? These are not idle questions. They are all-important, and without a qualified answer to them, our "what" is not well-specified. We will not know what we are aiming for in anything but the vaguest of terms.

In sum, we are left with two sub-projects in this grander project of clarifying the "what". Project 1 is the project of describing it in traditional ethical terms: what do we consider valuable in terms of conscious subjects and their states, such as happiness and suffering? Project 2 is the project of specifying, or perhaps rather understanding, what the terms we use in this first project refer to in physical terms: what kinds of physical structures mediate conscious subjects and their specific states, such as happiness and suffering?

Both these projects appear highly neglected among effective altruists, although there are a few who are devoting significant attention to them. Among the people associated with effective altruism who work on Project 1 are philosophers Hilary Greaves at the University of Oxford and Simon Knutsson at Stockholm University. And among those who work on Project 2 are Mike Johnson and Andrés Gómez Emilsson, who together have founded the Qualia Research Institute (QRI) with the purpose of making progress on it.[69] Another would be philosopher David Pearce, who argues that we should prioritize gaining a deeper understanding of the biological basis of suffering so that we can abolish it throughout the living world, what he calls the abolitionist project.[70]

---

[69] https://qualiaresearchinstitute.org/

[70] https://www.abolitionist.com/

Again, this project of value clarification cannot be perfectly precise, as we cannot specify the value of all possible, or even actual, physical states that are plausibly of moral relevance. Still, we may well be able to specify it precisely enough for most intents and purposes. Indeed, no matter what, it only seems reasonable to try to specify it as well as we can. The more precisely we specify it, the better we know what we are aiming for, and the better we can bring it about.

Zooming all the way out, we have seen that we have two very difficult, very different questions we need to answer as effective altruists, one concerning *what* is valuable, and another concerning *how* to best bring that "what" about. Our answers to both these questions are bound to be imprecise, yet we still need to be as precise and qualified about them as we can. In particular, with respect to the question of value, or clarifying what helping others means, we urgently need to have a deeper conversation and to do more research and reflection, since everything else, from the activism of today to the values we should implement in the AI of tomorrow, depends on our answer to it. In the hope of inspiring such a conversation, I shall try to lay out a rough account of the values I would favor in the following two chapters — my own preferred rough answers to Project 1.

SUFFERING-FOCUSED ETHICS

The view of values I would favor falls within a broader class of ethical views one may call suffering-focused ethics, which encompasses all views that give special priority to the alleviation and prevention of suffering. I will review some general arguments and considerations in favor of such views in this chapter, arguments that individually and collectively can support granting moral priority to suffering.[71] This general case will then be followed by a more specific case for a particular suffering-focused view — what I consider to be the strongest and most convincing one — in the next chapter.

It should be noted, however, that not all effective altruists agree with this view of values. Many appear to view the creation of happiness — for example, via the creation of new happy beings, or by raising the level of happiness of the already happy — as having the same importance as the

---

[71] This chapter is inspired by other resources that also advocate for suffering-focused ethics, such as the following:

https://foundational-research.org/the-case-for-suffering-focused-ethics/

https://www.utilitarianism.com/nu/nufaq.html

https://www.youtube.com/watch?v=4OWl5nTctYI

https://www.hedweb.com/negutil.htm

Pearce, 2017, part II

A more elaborate case for focusing on suffering can be found in Jamie Mayerfeld's *Suffering and Moral Responsibility*.

reduction of "equal" suffering. I used to hold this view as well. Yet I have changed my mind in light of considerations of the kind presented below.[72]

The Asymmetries

We have already briefly visited one asymmetry that seems to exist, at least in the eyes of many people, between suffering and happiness, namely the so-called Asymmetry in population ethics, which roughly says that we have an obligation to avoid bringing miserable lives into the world, but no obligation to bring about happy lives. To the extent we agree with this view, it appears that we agree that we should assign greater moral value and priority to the alleviation and prevention of suffering over the creation of happiness, at least in the context of the creation of new lives.

A similar view has been expressed by philosopher Jan Narveson, who has argued that there is value in making people happy, but not in making happy people.[73] Another philosopher who holds a similar view is Christoph Fehige, who defends a position he calls antifrustrationism, according to which we have obligations to make preferrers satisfied, but no obligations to make satisfied preferrers.[74] Peter Singer, too, has expressed a similar view in the past:

> The creation of preferences which we then satisfy gains us nothing. We can think of the creation of the unsatisfied preferences as putting a debit in the moral ledger which satisfying them merely cancels out. [...] Preference Utilitarians have grounds for seeking to satisfy their wishes, but they cannot say that the

---

[72] Not least have I changed my mind about whether a term like "equal suffering" is at all meaningful in general.

[73] Narveson, 1973.

[74] Fehige, 1998.

universe would have been a worse place if we had never come into existence at all.[75]

In terms of how we choose to prioritize our resources, there does indeed, to many of us at least, seem something highly unpalatable, not to say immoral and frivolous, about focusing on creating happiness de novo rather than on alleviating and preventing suffering first and foremost. As philosopher Adriano Mannino has expressed it:

> What's beyond my *comprehension* is why turning rocks into happiness elsewhere should matter at all. That strikes me as okay, but still utterly useless and therefore immoral if it comes at the opportunity cost of not preventing suffering. The non-creation of happiness is not problematic, for it never results in a problem for anyone (i.e. any consciousness-moment), and so there's never a problem you can point to in the world; the non-prevention of suffering, on the other hand, results in a problem.[76]

And in the case of extreme suffering, one can argue that the word "problem" is a strong contender for most understated euphemism in history. Mannino's view can be said to derive from what is arguably an intuitive and common-sense "understanding of ethics as being about solving the world's problems: We confront spacetime, see wherever there is or will be a problem, i.e. a struggling being, and we solve it."[77]

---

[75] Singer, 1980b. However, Singer goes on to say about this view of coming into existence that it "perhaps, is a reason to combine [preference and hedonistic utilitarianism]". Furthermore, Singer seems to have moved much closer toward, and to now defend, hedonistic utilitarianism, whereas he was arguably primarily a preference utilitarian when he made the quoted statement.

[76] Quoted from a Facebook conversation.

[77] https://foundational-research.org/the-case-for-suffering-focused-ethics/

Simon Knutsson has expressed a similar sentiment to the opportunity cost consideration expressed by Mannino above, and highlighted the crucial juxtaposition we must consider:

> When spending resources on increasing the number of beings instead of preventing extreme suffering, one is essentially saying to the victims: "I could have helped you, but I didn't, because I think it's more important that individuals are brought into existence. Sorry."[78]

Philosopher David Benatar defends an asymmetry much stronger than the aforementioned Asymmetry in population ethics, as he argues that we not only should avoid bringing (overtly) miserable lives into existence, but that we ideally should avoid bringing any lives into existence at all, since coming into existence is always a harm on Benatar's account. Explained simply, Benatar's main argument rests on the premise that the absence of suffering is good, while the absence of happiness is not bad, and hence the state of non-existence is good ("good" + "not bad" = "good"), whereas the presence of suffering and happiness is bad and good respectively, and hence not a pure good, which renders it worse than the state of non-existence according to Benatar.[79]

Beyond this asymmetry, Benatar further argues that there is an asymmetry in how much suffering and happiness our lives contain — e.g. that the worst forms of suffering are far worse than the best pleasures are good; that we almost always experience some subtle unpleasantness, dissatisfaction, and preference frustration; and that there are such negative things as chronic pain, impairment, and trauma, yet no corresponding

---

[78] http://www.simonknutsson.com/the-one-paragraph-case-for-suffering-focused-ethics

[79] Benatar, 2006, chapter 2.

positive things, like chronic pleasure.[80] And the reason that we fail to acknowledge this, Benatar argues, is that we have various, well-documented psychological biases which cause us to evaluate our lives in overly optimistic terms.[81]

It seems worth expanding a bit on this more quantitative asymmetry between the respective badness and goodness of suffering and happiness. For even if one rejects the notion that there is a qualitative difference between the moral status of creating happiness and preventing suffering — e.g. that a failure to prevent suffering is problematic, while a failure to create happiness is not — it seems difficult to deny Benatar's claim that the worst forms of suffering are far worse than the best of pleasures are good. Imagine, for example, that we were offered ten years of the greatest happiness possible on the condition that we must undergo some amount of hellish torture in order to get it. How much torture would we be willing to endure in order to get this prize? Many of us would reject the offer completely and prefer a non-existent, entirely non-problematic state over any mixture of hellish torture and heavenly happiness.

Others, however, will be willing to accept the offer and make a sacrifice. And the question is then how big a sacrifice one could reasonably be willing to make? Seconds of hellish torture? A full hour? Perhaps even an entire day? Some might go as far as saying an entire day, yet it seems that no matter how much one values happiness, no one could reasonably push the scale to anywhere near 50/50. That is, no one could reasonably choose to endure ten years of hellish torture in order to attain ten years of sublime happiness.

Those who would be willing to endure a full day of torture in order to enjoy ten years of paradise are, I think, among those who are willing to

---

[80] Benatar, 2006, chapter 3.

[81] Benatar, 2006, chapter 3.

push it the furthest in order to attain such happiness, and yet notice how far they are from 50/50. We are not talking 80/20, 90/10, or even 99/1 here. No, one day of hell for 3650 days of paradise roughly corresponds to a "days of happiness to days of suffering" ratio of 99.97 to 0.03. And that is for those who are willing to push it. [82]

So not only is there no symmetry here; the moral weight of the worst of suffering appears to be orders of magnitude greater than that of the greatest happiness, which implies that the prevention of suffering appears the main name of the ethical game on any plausible moral calculus. Even on a view according to which we are willing to really push it and endure what is, arguably by most accounts, an unreasonable amount of suffering in order to gain happiness, the vast majority of moral weight is *still* found in preventing suffering, at least when speaking in terms of durations of the best and worst potential states. And one can reasonably argue that this is also true of the actual state of the world, as Arthur Schopenhauer did when comparing "the feelings of an animal engaged in eating another with those of the animal being eaten." [83]

A more general and qualitative asymmetry between the moral status of happiness and suffering has been defended by philosopher Karl Popper:

I believe that there is, from the ethical point of view, no symmetry between suffering and happiness, or between pain and pleasure.

---

[82] One may object that our choosing such a skewed trade-off is merely a reflection of our contingent biology, and that it may be possible to create happiness so great that most people would consider a single day of it worth ten years of the worst kinds of suffering our biology can support. To this I would respond that such a possibility remains hypothetical, indeed speculative, and that we should base our views mainly on the actualities we know rather than such hypothetical (and wishful) possibilities. After all, it may also be, indeed it seems about equally likely, that suffering can be far worse than the worst suffering our contingent biology can support, and, furthermore, it may be that the pattern familiar from our contingent biology only repeats itself in this realm of theoretical maxima; i.e. that such maximal suffering can only be deemed far more disvaluable than the greatest bliss possible can be deemed valuable.

[83] Schopenhauer, 1851/1970, p. 42.

[...] In my opinion human suffering makes a direct moral appeal, namely, the appeal for help, while there is no similar call to increase the happiness of a man who is doing well anyway. A further criticism of the Utilitarian formula "Maximize pleasure" is that it assumes a continuous pleasure-pain scale which allows us to treat degrees of pain as negative degrees of pleasure. But, from the moral point of view, pain cannot be outweighed by pleasure, and especially not one man's pain by another man's pleasure. Instead of the greatest happiness for the greatest number, one should demand, more modestly, the least amount of avoidable suffering for all; [...][84]

David Pearce, who identifies as a negative utilitarian, describes his view in a similar way:

Ethical negative-utilitarianism is a value-system which challenges the moral symmetry of pleasure and pain. It doesn't question the value of enhancing the happiness of the already happy. Yet it attaches value in a distinctively *moral* sense of the term only to actions which tend to minimise or eliminate suffering. This is what matters above all else.[85]

Neither Popper nor Pearce appear to deny that there is value in happiness. Instead, what they deny is that the value there may be in creating happiness is comparable to the value of reducing suffering. In Pearce's words, increasing the happiness of the already happy does not carry value in the distinctively moral sense that reducing suffering does; in Popper's

---

[84] Popper, 1945/2011, note 2 to chapter 9.

[85] https://www.hedweb.com/negutil.htm

words, suffering makes a direct moral appeal for help, while the state of those who are doing well does not.

Expressed in other words, one may say that the difference is that suffering, by its very nature, carries urgency, whereas the creation of happiness does not, at least not in a similar way. (Popper put it similarly: "[…] the promotion of happiness is in any case much less urgent than the rendering of help to those who suffer […]"[86]) We would rightly rush to send an ambulance to help someone who is enduring extreme suffering, yet not to boost the happiness of someone who is already happy, no matter how much we may be able to boost it. Similarly, if we had pills that could raise the happiness of those who are already doing well to the greatest heights possible, there would be no urgency in distributing these pills (to those already doing well), whereas if a single person fell to the ground in unbearable agony right before us, there would indeed be an urgency to help. Increasing the happiness of the already happy is, unlike the alleviation of extreme suffering, not an emergency.

A similar consideration about David Pearce's abolitionist project described in the previous chapter — the abolition of suffering throughout the living world via biotechnology — appears to lend credence to this asymmetrical view of the moral status of the creation of happiness versus the prevention of suffering. For imagine we had completed the abolitionist project and made suffering non-existent for good. The question is then whether it can reasonably be maintained that our moral obligations would be exactly the same after this completion. Would we have an equally strong duty or obligation to move sentience to new heights after we had abolished suffering? Or would we instead have discharged our prime moral obligation, and thus have reason to lower our shoulders and breathe a deep and justified sigh of moral relief? I think the latter.

---

[86] Popper, 1945/2011, note 6 to chapter 5.

Another reason in favor of an asymmetrical view is that, echoing Benatar somewhat, it seems that the absence of extreme happiness cannot be considered bad in remotely the same way that the absence of extreme suffering can be considered good. For example, if a person is in a state of dreamless sleep rather than having the experience of a lifetime, this cannot reasonably be characterized as a disaster or a catastrophe; the difference between these two states does not seem to carry great moral weight. Yet when it comes to the difference between sleeping and being tortured, we are indeed talking about a difference that does carry immense moral weight, and the realization of the worse rather than the better outcome would indeed amount to a catastrophe.

The final asymmetry I shall review in this section is one that is found more on a meta-level, namely in the distribution of views concerning the moral value of the creation of happiness and the prevention of suffering. For in our broader human conversation about what has value, very few seem to have seriously disputed the disvalue of suffering and the importance of preventing it. Indeed, to the extent that we can find a value that almost everyone agrees on, it is this: suffering matters. In contrast, there are many who have disputed the value and importance of creating more happiness, including many of the philosophers mentioned in this section; many thinkers in Eastern philosophy for whom moksha, liberation from suffering, is the highest good; as well as many thinkers in Western philosophy, with roots all the way back to Epicurus, for whom ataraxia, an untroubled state free from distress, was the highest aim. Further elaboration on a version of this view of happiness follows in the next section.

This asymmetry in consensus about the value and moral status of creating happiness versus preventing suffering also counts as a weak reason for giving greater priority to the latter.

Tranquilism: Happiness as the Absence of Suffering

Author Lukas Gloor defends a view he calls tranquilism, which — following Epicurus and his notion of ataraxia, as well as the goal of moksha proposed as the highest good by many Eastern philosophers[87] — holds that the value of happiness lies in its absence of suffering.[88] Thus, according to tranquilism, states of euphoric bliss are not of greater value than, say, states of peaceful contentment free of any negative components. Or, for that matter, than a similarly undisturbed state of dreamless sleep or insentience. In other words, states of happiness are of equal value to nothing, provided that they are shorn of suffering.

In this way, tranquilism is well in line with the asymmetry in moral status between happiness and suffering defended by Karl Popper and David Pearce: that increasing the happiness of the already happy does not have the moral value that reducing suffering does. And one may even argue that it explains this asymmetry: if the value of happiness lies in its absence of suffering, then it follows that creating happiness (for those not suffering) cannot take precedence over reducing suffering. Moving someone from zero to (another kind of) zero can never constitute a greater move on the value scale than moving someone from a negative state to a (however marginally) less negative one.[89]

---

[87] Some version of the concept of moksha is central to most of the well-known Eastern traditions, such as Buddhism (nirvana), Hinduism, Jainism, and Sikhism (mukti).

[88] https://foundational-research.org/tranquilism/

Thus, the view is not that happiness is literally the absence of suffering, which is, of course, patently false — insentient rocks are obviously not happy — but rather that *the value of* happiness lies in its absence of suffering.

[89] It should be noted, however, that one need not hold this tranquilist view of value in order to

agree with Popper's and Pearce's position. For example, one can also view happiness as being strictly more valuable than nothing, while still maintaining that the value of raising the happiness of the already happy is always less than the value of reducing suffering. An intuitive way of formalizing this view would be by representing the value of states of suffering with negative real numbers, while representing the value of states of pure happiness with hyperreal numbers greater than 0, yet smaller than any positive real number, allowing us to assign some

To many of us, this is a highly counter-intuitive view, at least at first sight. After all, do we not seek pleasure almost all the time, often at the seemingly justified cost of suffering? Yet one can frame this seeking in another way that is consistent with tranquilism, by viewing our search for pleasure as really being an attempt to escape suffering and dissatisfaction. On this framing, what appears to be going from neutral to positive is really going from a state of negativity, however subtle, to a state that is relieved, at least to some extent, from this negativity. So, on this view, when we visit a friend we have desired to see for some time, we do not go from a neutral to a positive state, but instead just remove our craving for their company and the dissatisfaction caused by their absence. So too with the pleasure of physical exercise: it is liberating in that it gives us temporary freedom from the bad feelings and moods that follow from not exercising. Or even the pleasure of falling in love, which provides refreshing relief from the boredom and desire we are otherwise plagued by.

Psychologist William James seemed to agree with this view of happiness:

> Happiness, I have lately discovered, is no positive feeling, but a negative condition of freedom from a number of restrictive sensations of which our organism usually seems the seat. When they are wiped out, the clearness and cleanness of the contrast is happiness. This is why anaesthetics make us so happy.[90]

As did Arthur Schopenhauer:

---

states of pure happiness greater value than others. On tranquilism, by contrast, all states of (pure) happiness would be assigned exactly the value 0.

[90] James, 1901.

[...] evil is precisely that which is positive,[91] that which makes itself palpable, and good, on the other hand, i.e. all happiness and gratification, is that which is negative, the mere abolition of a desire and extinction of a pain.[92]

And here is how Lukas Gloor explains it:

> In the context of everyday life, there are almost always things that ever so slightly bother us. Uncomfortable pressure in the shoes, thirst, hunger, headaches, boredom, itches, non-effortless work, worries, longing for better times. When our brain is flooded with pleasure, we temporarily become unaware of all the negative ingredients of our stream of consciousness, and they thus cease to exist. Pleasure is the typical way in which our minds experience temporary freedom from suffering, which may contribute to the view that happiness is the symmetrical counterpart to suffering, and that pleasure, at the expense of all other possible states, is intrinsically important and worth bringing about.[93]

One may object that the implication that mere contentment has the same value as the greatest euphoric bliss seems implausible, and thus counts against tranquilism. Yet whether this is indeed implausible depends on the eyes that look. For consider it this way: if someone who experiences "mere contentment" without any negative cravings[94] whatsoever, and thus

---

[91] The terms "positive" and "negative" here respectively refer to the presence and absence of something.

[92] Schopenhauer, 1851/1970, p. 41.

[93] https://foundational-research.org/tranquilism/

[94] I happen to disagree with Gloor's particular formulation of tranquilism when he writes: "According to tranquilism, a state of consciousness is negative or disvaluable if and only if it

does not find the experience insufficient in any way, who are we to say that they are wrong about their state, and that they actually should want something better? Tranquilism denies that such a "merely content" person is wrong to claim that their state is perfect. Indeed, tranquilism is here in perfect agreement with this person, and hence this implication of tranquilism is at least not implausible from this person's perspective, which one may argue is the most relevant perspective to consider in this context of discussing whether said person is in a suboptimal state. The perspective from which this implication appears implausible, a proponent of tranquilism may argue, is only from the perspective of someone who is not in perfect contentment — one who desires euphoric bliss, for oneself and others, and in some sense feels lacking, i.e. a negative craving, about its absence.

Another apparent, and perhaps intuitive, reason to reject tranquilism is that it appears to imply that happiness is not really that wonderful — that the best experience one has ever had was not really that great. Yet it is important to make clear that tranquilism implies no such thing. On the contrary, according to tranquilism, experiences of happiness without any suffering are indeed (together with other experiential states that are absent of suffering) experiences of the most wonderful kind, and they are by no means less wonderful than they are felt. What tranquilism *does* say, however, is that the value of such states is due to their absence of suffering, and that the creation of such happy states cannot justify the creation of suffering.

Yet even so, even while allowing us to maintain the view that happiness is wonderful, tranquilism is still, at least for many of us, really not a nice way to think about the world, and about the nature of value in particular, as we would probably all like to think that there exists

contains a craving for change." For it seems to me that even intense cravings for change (for a different sex position, say) can feel perfectly fine and non-negative; that euphoric desire, say, is not an oxymoron. The term "negative cravings" avoids this complication.

something of truly positive value in the realm of conscious experience beyond merely the absence of negative experiences or cravings. Yet this want of ours — this negative craving, one could say — should only make us that much more skeptical of any reluctance we may have to give tranquilism a fair hearing. And even if, upon doing so, one does not find tranquilism an entirely convincing or exhaustive account of the respective (dis)value of happiness and suffering, it seems difficult to deny that there is a significant grain of truth to it.

The implications of tranquilism are clear: creating more happiness (for the currently non-existent or otherwise not suffering) has neutral value, while there *is* value in the alleviation and prevention of suffering, a value that, as noted above, nobody seriously questions.

Creating Happiness at the Cost of Suffering Is Wrong

In this section I shall not argue for a novel, separate point, but instead invoke some concrete examples that help make the case for a particular claim that follows directly from many of the views we have seen above, the claim being that it is wrong to create happiness at the cost of suffering.

One obvious example of such gratuitous suffering would be that of torturing a single person for the enjoyment of a large crowd.[95] If we think happiness can always outweigh suffering, we seem forced to say that, yes, provided that the resulting enjoyment of the crowd is great enough, and if other things are equal, then such happiness can indeed outweigh and justify torturing a single person. Yet that seems misguided.

A similar example to consider is that of a gang rape: if we think happiness can always outweigh suffering, then such a rape can in principle be justified, provided that the pleasure of the rapists is sufficiently great. Yet most people would find this proposition utterly wrong.

---

[95] The similar case of forcing gladiators to fight for the enjoyment of a full colosseum is often raised as a problematic case for (certain versions of) utilitarianism.

One may object that these thought experiments bring other issues into play than merely that of happiness versus suffering, which is a fair point. Yet we can in a sense control for these by reversing the purpose of these acts so that they are about reducing suffering rather than increasing happiness for a given group of individuals. So rather than the torture of a single person being done for the enjoyment of a crowd, it is now done in order to prevent a crowd from being tortured; rather than the rape being done for the pleasure of, say, five people, it is done to prevent five people from being raped. While we may still find it most unpalatable to give the go signal for such preventive actions, it nonetheless seems clear that torturing a single person in order to prevent the torture of many people would be the right thing to do, and that having less rape occur is better than having more.

A similar example, which however does not involve any extreme suffering, is the situation described in Ursula K. Le Guin's short story *The Ones Who Walk Away from Omelas*. The story is about an almost utopian city, Omelas, in which everyone lives an extraordinarily happy and meaningful life, except for a single child who is locked in a basement room, fated to live a life of squalor:

> The child used to scream for help at night, and cry a good deal, but now it only makes a kind of whining, "eh-haa, eh-haa," and it speaks less and less often. It is so thin there are no calves to its legs; its belly protrudes; it lives on a half-bowl of corn meal and grease a day. It is naked. Its buttocks and thighs are a mass of festered sores, as it sits in its own excrement continually.[96]

---

[96] Guin, 1973/1992.

The story ends by describing some people in the city who appear to find the situation unacceptable and who choose not to take part in it any more — the ones who walk away from Omelas.

The relevant question for us to consider here is whether we would walk away from Omelas, or perhaps rather whether we would choose to bring a condition like Omelas into existence in the first place. Can the happy and meaningful lives of the other people in Omelas justify the existence of this single, miserable child? Different people have different intuitions about it; some will say that it depends on how many people live in Omelas. Yet to many of us, the answer is "no" — the creation of happiness is comparatively frivolous and unnecessary, and it cannot justify the creation of such a victim, of such misery and suffering.[97] A sentiment to the same effect was expressed in the novel *The Plague*, by Albert Camus: "For who would dare to assert that eternal happiness can compensate for a single moment's human suffering?"[98]

A "no" to the creation of Omelas would also be supported by the Asymmetry in population ethics, according to which it has neutral value to add a happy life to Omelas, while adding this one miserable child has negative value, and hence the net value of the creation of Omelas is negative.

The examples visited above all argue for the claim that it is wrong to impose certain forms of suffering on someone for the sake of creating happiness, where the forms of suffering have gradually been decreasing in severity. And one may argue that the plausibility of the claims these respective examples have been used to support has been decreasing

---

[97] And even though many will probably insist that the child's suffering is a worthy sacrifice, the fact that it only takes a single life of misery to bring the value of a whole paradisiacal city into serious question, as it seems to do for most people, is yet another strong hint that there is an asymmetry between the (dis)value of happiness and suffering.

[98] Camus, 1947/1991, p. 224.

gradually too, and for this very reason: the less extreme the suffering, the less clear it is that happiness could never outweigh it. And yet even in the case of the imposition of the mildest of suffering — a pinprick, say — for the sake of the creation of happiness, it is far from clear, upon closer examination, that this should be deemed permissible, much less an ethical obligation. Echoing the passage by Camus above, would it really be right to impose a pinprick on someone in order to create pleasure for ourselves or others, or indeed for the very person we do it on, provided that whomever would gain the happiness is doing perfectly fine already, and thus that the resulting happiness would not in fact amount to a reduction of suffering? Looking only at, or rather from, the perspective of that moment's suffering itself, the act would indeed be bad, and the question is then what could justify such badness, given that the alternative was an entirely trouble-free state. If one holds that being ethical means to promote happiness *over* suffering, not to create happiness *at the cost of* suffering, the answer is "nothing".

Two Objections

Finally, it is worth briefly addressing two common objections against suffering-focused ethics, the first one being that not many people have held such a view, which makes it appear implausible. The first thing to say in response to this claim is that, even if it were true, the fact that a position is not widely held is not a strong reason to consider it implausible, especially if one thinks one has strong, object-level reasons to consider it plausible, and, furthermore, if one believes there are human biases[99] that can readily explain its (purportedly) widespread rejection. The second thing to say is that the claim is simply not true, as there are many thinkers, historical as well as contemporary ones, who have defended views similar

---

[99] Cf. Benatar, 2006, chapter 3.

to those outlined here (see the following note for examples).[100]

Another objection is that suffering-focused views have unappealing consequences, including that, according to such views, it would be right to kill everyone (or "destroy the world"). One reply to this claim is that at least some suffering-focused views do not have this implication. For example, in his book *The Battle for Compassion: Ethics in an Apathetic Universe*, Jonathan Leighton argues for a pragmatic position he calls "negative utilitarianism plus", according to which we should aim to do our best to reduce preventable suffering, yet where we can still "categorically refuse to intentionally destroy the planet and eliminate ourselves and everything we care about in the process [...]".[101]

Another reply is that, as Simon Knutsson has argued at greater length,[102] other ethical views that have a consequentialist component seem about as vulnerable to similar objections. For instance, if maximizing the sum of happiness minus suffering were our core objective, it could be said that we ought to kill people in order to replace them with happier beings. One may then object, quite reasonably, that this is unlikely to be optimal in practice, yet one can argue — as reasonably, I believe — that the same holds true of trying to destroy the world in order to reduce suffering: it does not seem the best we can do in practice. I shall say a bit more about this last point in the penultimate chapter on future directions.

Having visited this general case for suffering-focused ethics, we shall now turn to what is arguably the strongest case for such a view — the appeal to sympathy for intense suffering.

---

[100] See section 2.2.14 here https://www.utilitarianism.com/nu/nufaq.html as well as http://www.simonknutsson.com/thoughts-on-ords-why-im-not-a-negative-utilitarian

[101] Leighton, 2011, p. 96.

[102] http://www.simonknutsson.com/the-world-destruction-argument/

THE PRINCIPLE OF SYMPATHY
FOR INTENSE SUFFERING

The ethical view I would advocate most strongly is a suffering-focused view that centers on a core principle of Sympathy for Intense Suffering, or SIS for short, which roughly holds that we should prioritize the interests of those who are, or will be, in a state of extreme suffering. In particular: that we should prioritize their interest in avoiding such suffering higher than anything else.[103]

One can say that this view takes its point of departure in classical utilitarianism, the theory that we should maximize the net sum of happiness minus suffering. Yet it questions a tacit assumption, a particular existence claim, often held in conjunction with the classical utilitarian framework, namely that for every instance of suffering, there exists some amount of happiness that can outweigh it.

This is a deeply problematic assumption, in my view. More than that, it is peculiar that classical utilitarianism seems widely believed to entail this assumption, given that (to my knowledge) none of the seminal

---

[103] This view is similar to what Brian Tomasik calls consent-based negative utilitarianism:
http://reducing-suffering.org/happiness-suffering-symmetric/#Consent-based_negative_utilitarianism
And the Organisation for the Prevention of Intense Suffering (OPIS) appears founded upon a virtually identical principle: http://www.preventsuffering.org/
I do not claim that this view is original; merely that it is important.

classical utilitarians — Jeremy Bentham, John Stuart Mill, and Henry Sidgwick — ever argued for this existence claim, or even discussed it. [104] Thus, it seems that the acceptance of this assumption is no more entailed by classical utilitarianism, defined as the ethical view, or views, expressed by these utilitarian philosophers, than is its rejection.

The question of whether this assumption is reasonable ties into a deeper discussion about how to measure and weigh happiness and suffering against each other, and I think this is much less well-defined than is commonly supposed (even though the trickiness of the task is often acknowledged). [105] The problem is that we have a common sense view that goes something like the following: if a conscious subject deems some state of suffering worth experiencing in order to attain some given pleasure, then this pleasure is worth the suffering. And this common sense view may work for most of us most of the time. [106] Yet it runs into problems in cases where the subject deems their suffering so unbearable that no amount of happiness could ever outweigh it.

For what would the common sense view say in such a situation? That the suffering indeed cannot be outweighed by any pleasure? That would seem an intuitive suggestion, yet the problem is that we can also imagine the case of an experience of some pleasure that the subject, in that

---

[104] And I have read them all, though admittedly not their complete works. Bentham can seem to come close in chapter 4 of his *Principles of Morals and Legislation*, where he outlines a method for measuring pain and pleasure. One of the steps of this method consists in summing up the values of "[…] all the pleasures on one side and of all the pains on the other." And later he writes of this process that it is "[…] applicable to pleasure and pain in whatever form they appear […]". Yet he does not write that the sum will necessarily be finite, nor, more specifically, whether every instance of suffering necessarily can be outweighed by some pleasure. I suspect Bentham, as well as Mill and Sidgwick, never contemplated this question in the first place.

[105] A recommendable essay on the issue is Simon Knutsson's "Measuring Happiness and Suffering": https://foundational-research.org/measuring-happiness-and-suffering/

[106] However, a defender of tranquilism would, of course, question whether we are indeed talking about a pleasure outweighing some suffering rather than it, upon closer examination, really being a case of a reduction of some form of suffering outweighing some other form of suffering

experience-moment, deems so great that it can outweigh even the worst forms of suffering, which leaves us with mutually incompatible value claims (although it is worth noting that one can reasonably doubt the existence of such positive states, whereas, as we shall see below, the existence of correspondingly negative experiences is a certainty).[107] How are we to evaluate these claims?

The aforementioned common sense method of evaluation has clearly broken down at this point, and is entirely silent on the matter. We are forced to appeal to another principle of evaluation. And the principle I would argue we should employ is, as hinted above, to choose to sympathize with those who are worst off — those who are experiencing intense suffering. Hence the principle of sympathy for intense suffering: we should sympathize with, and prioritize, the evaluations of those subjects who deem their suffering unoutweighable, even if only for a brief experience-moment, and thus give total priority to helping these subjects. More precisely, we should minimize the amount of such experience-moments of extreme suffering. That, on this account of value, is the greatest help we can do for others.[108]

---

[107] And therefore, if one assumes a framework of so-called moral uncertainty, it seems that one should assign much greater plausibility to negative value lexicality than to positive value lexicality (cf. https://foundational-research.org/value-lexicality/), also in light of the point made in the previous chapter that many have doubted the positive value of happiness (as being due to anything but its absence of suffering), whereas virtually nobody has seriously doubted the disvalue of suffering.

[108] But what if there are several levels of extreme suffering, where an experience on each level is deemed so bad that no amount of experiences on a lower level could outweigh it? This is a tricky issue, yet to the extent that these levels of badness are ordered such that, say, no amount of level I suffering can outweigh a single instance of level II suffering (according to a subject who has experienced both), then I would argue that we should give priority to reducing level II suffering. Yet what if level I suffering is found to be worse than level II suffering in the moment of experiencing it, while level II suffering is found to be worse than level I suffering when *it* is experienced? One may then say that the evaluation should be up to some third experience-moment with memory of both states, and that we should trust such an evaluation, or, if this is not possible, we may view both forms of suffering as equally bad. Whether such dilemmas arise in the real world, and how to best resolve them in case they do, stands to me as an open question.

This principle actually seems to have a lot of support from common sense and "common wisdom". For example, imagine two children are offered to ride a roller coaster, one of whom would find the ride very pleasant, while the other child would find it very *un*pleasant, and imagine, furthermore, that the only two options available are that they either both ride or neither of them ride (and if neither of them ride, they are both perfectly fine).[109] Whose interests should we sympathize with and favor? Common sense would appear to favor the child who would not want to take the ride. The mere pleasure of the "ride-positive" child does not justify a violation of the interest of the other child not to suffer a very unpleasant experience. The interest in not enduring such suffering seems far more fundamental, and hence to have ethical primacy, compared to the relatively trivial and frivolous interest of having a very pleasant experience.[110]

Arguably, common sense even suggests the same in the case where there are many more children who would find the ride very pleasant, while still only one child who would find it very unpleasant (provided, again, that the children will all be perfectly fine if they do not ride). Indeed, I believe a significant fraction of people would say the same no matter how many such "ride-positive" children we put on the scale: it would still be wrong to give them the ride at the cost of forcing the "ride-negative" child to undergo the very unpleasant experience.[111]

Thus, cf. the point about the lack of clarity and specification of values we saw two chapters ago, the framework I present here is not only not perfectly specific, as it surely cannot be, but it is admittedly quite far from it indeed. Nonetheless, it still comprises a significant step in the direction of carving out a clearer set of values, much clearer than the core value of, say, "reducing suffering".

[109] A similar example is often used by the suffering-focused advocate Inmendham.

[110] This is, of course, essentially the same claim we saw a case for in the previous chapter: that creating happiness at the cost of suffering is wrong. The principle advocated here may be considered a special case of this claim, namely the special case where the suffering in question is deemed irredeemably bad by the subject.

And yet the suffering in this example — a very unpleasant experience on a roller coaster — can hardly be said to count as remotely extreme, much less an instance of the worst forms of suffering; the forms of suffering that constitute the strongest, and in my view overwhelming, case for the principle of sympathy for intense suffering. Such intense suffering, even if balanced against the most intense forms of pleasure imaginable, only demands even stronger relative sympathy and priority. However bad we may consider the imposition of a very unpleasant experience for the sake of a very pleasant one, the imposition of extreme suffering for the sake of extreme pleasure must be deemed far worse.

The Horrendous Support for SIS

The worst forms of suffering are so terrible that merely thinking about them for a brief moment can leave the average sympathetic person in a state of horror and darkness for a good while, and therefore, quite naturally, we strongly prefer not to contemplate these things. Yet if we are to make sure that we have our priorities right, and that our views about what matters most in this world are as well-considered as possible, then we cannot shy away from the task of contemplating and trying to appreciate the disvalue of these worst of horrors. This is no easy task, and not just because we are reluctant to think about the issue in the first place, but also because it is difficult to gain anything close to a true appreciation of the reality in question. As David Pearce put it:

---

[111] Cf. the gut feeling many people seem to have that the scenario described in *The Ones Who Walk Away from Omelas* should not be brought into the world regardless of how big the city of Omelas would be. Weak support for this claim is also found in the following survey, in which a plurality of people said that they think future civilization should strive to minimize suffering (over, for instance, maximizing positive experiences): https://futureoflife.org/superintelligence-survey/

It's easy to convince oneself that things can't *really* be that bad, that the horror invoked is being overblown, that what is going on elsewhere in space-time is somehow less real than *this* here-and-now, or that the good in the world somehow offsets the bad. Yet however vividly one thinks one can imagine what agony, torture or suicidal despair must be like, the reality is inconceivably worse. Hazy images of Orwell's 'Room 101' barely hint at what I'm talking about. The force of 'inconceivably' is itself largely inconceivable here.[112]

Nonetheless, we can still gain at least some, admittedly rather limited, appreciation by considering some real-world examples of extreme suffering (what follows are examples of an extremely unpleasant character that may be triggering and traumatizing).

One such example is the tragic fate of the Japanese girl Junko Furuta who was kidnapped in 1988, at the age of 16, by four teenage boys. According to their own trial statements, the boys raped her hundreds of times; "inserted foreign objects, such as iron bars, scissors and skewers into her vagina and anus, rendering her unable to defecate and urinate properly"; "beat her several times with golf clubs, bamboo sticks and iron rods"; "used her as a punching bag by hanging her body from the ceiling"; "dropped barbells onto her stomach several times"; "set fireworks into her

---

[112] https://www.hedweb.com/negutil.htm

A personal anecdote of mine in support of Pearce's quote is that I tend to write and talk a lot about reducing suffering, and yet I am *always* unpleasantly surprised by how bad it is when I experience even just borderline intense suffering. I then always get the sense that I have absolutely no idea what I am talking about when I am talking about suffering in my usual happy state, although the words I use in that state are quite accurate: that it is really bad. In those bad states I realize that it is *far* worse than we tend to think, even when we think it is really, really bad. It truly is inconceivable, as Pearce writes, since we simply cannot simulate that badness in a remotely faithful way when we are feeling good, quite analogously to the phenomenon of binocular rivalry, where we can only perceive one of two visual images at a time.

anus, vagina, mouth and ear"; "burnt her vagina and clitoris with cigarettes and lighters"; "tore off her left nipple with pliers"; and more. Eventually, she was no longer able to move from the ground, and she repeatedly begged the boys to kill her, which they eventually did, after 44 days.[113]

An example of extreme suffering that is much more common, indeed something that happens countless times every single day, is being eaten alive, a process that can sometimes last several hours with the victim still fully conscious of being devoured, muscle by muscle, organ by organ. A harrowing example of such a death that was caught on camera (see the following note) involved a baboon tearing apart the hind legs of a baby gazelle and eating this poor individual who remained conscious for longer than one would have thought and hoped possible.[114] A few minutes of a much more protracted such painful and horrifying death can be seen via the link in the following note (lions eating a baby elephant alive).[115] And a similar, yet quicker death of a man can be seen via the link in the following note.[116] Tragically, the man's wife and two children were sitting in a car next to him while it happened, yet they were unable to help him, and knowing this probably made the man's experience even more horrible, which ties into a point made by Simon Knutsson:

> Sometimes when the badness or moral importance of torture is discussed, it is described in terms of different stimuli that cause tissue damage, such as burning, cutting or stretching. But one

---

[113] https://ripeace.wordpress.com/2012/09/14/the-murder-of-junko-furuta-44-days-of-hell/
https://en.wikipedia.org/wiki/Murder_of_Junko_Furuta

[114] https://www.youtube.com/watch?v=PcnH_TOqi3I

[115] https://www.youtube.com/watch?v=Lc63Rp-UN10

[116] https://www.abolitionist.com/reprogramming/maneaters.html

should also remember different ways to make someone feel bad, and different kinds of bad feelings, which can be combined to make one's overall experience even more terrible. It is arguably the overall unpleasantness of one's experience that matters most in this context.[117]

After giving a real-world example with several layers of extreme cruelty and suffering combined, Knutsson goes on to write:

Although this example is terrible, one can imagine how it could be worse if more types of violence and bad feelings were added to the mix. To take another example: [Brian] Tomasik often talks about the Brazen bull as a particularly bad form of torture. The victim is locked inside a metal bull, a fire is lit underneath the bull and the victim is fried to death. It is easy to imagine how this can be made worse. For example, inject the victim with chemicals that amplify pain and block the body's natural pain inhibitors, and put her loved ones in the bull so that when she is being fried, she also sees her loved ones being fried. One can imagine further combinations that make it even worse. Talking only of stimuli such as burning almost trivializes how bad experiences can be.[118]

Another example of extreme suffering is what happened to Dax Cowart. In 1973, at the age of 25, Dax went on a trip with his father to visit land that he considered buying. Unfortunately, due to a pipeline leak, the air over the land was filled with propane gas, which is highly flammable when combined with oxygen. As they started their car, the propane ignited, and

---

[117] http://www.simonknutsson.com/the-seriousness-of-suffering-supplement

[118] http://www.simonknutsson.com/the-seriousness-of-suffering-supplement

the two men found themselves in a burning inferno. Dax's father died, and Dax himself had much of his hands, eyes, and ears burned away; two thirds of his skin was severely burned.[119]

The case of Dax has since become quite famous, not only, or even mainly, because of the extreme horror he experienced during this explosion, but because of the ethical issues raised by his treatment, which turned out to be about as torturous as the explosion itself. For Dax himself repeatedly said, immediately after the explosion as well as for months later, that he wanted to die more than anything else, and that he did not want to be subjected to any treatment that would keep him alive. Nonetheless, he was forcibly treated for a period of ten months, during which he tried to take his life several times.

Since then, Dax has managed to recover and live what he considers a happy life — he successfully sued the oil company responsible for the pipeline leak, which left him financially secure; he earned a law degree; and got married. Yet even so, he still wishes that he had been killed rather than treated. In Dax's own view, no happiness could ever compensate for what he went through.[120]

This kind of evaluation is exactly what the ethical principle advocated here centers on, and what the principle amounts to is simply a refusal to claim that Dax's evaluation, or any other like it, is wrong. It maintains that we should not allow the occurrence of such extreme horrors for the sake of any intrinsic good, and hence that we should prioritize alleviating and preventing them over anything else.[121]

---

[119] Dax describes the accident himself in the following video:

https://www.youtube.com/watch?v=M3ZnFJGmoq8

[120] Brülde, 2010, p. 576; Benatar, 2006, p. 63.

[121] And if one thinks such extreme suffering can be outweighed, an important question to ask oneself is: what exactly does it mean to say that it can be outweighed? More specifically, according to whom, and measured by what criteria, can such suffering be outweighed? The only promising option open, it seems, is to choose to prioritize the assessments of beings who say

One may object that the examples above do not all comprise clear cases where the suffering subject deems their suffering so bad that nothing could ever outweigh it. And more generally, one may object that there can exist intense suffering that is not necessarily deemed so bad that nothing could outweigh it, either because the subject is not able to make such an evaluation, or because the subject just chooses not to evaluate it that way. What would the principle of sympathy for intense suffering say about such cases? It would say the following: in cases where the suffering is intense, yet the sufferers choose not to deem it so bad that nothing could outweigh it (we may call this "red suffering"), we should prioritize reducing suffering of the kind that would be deemed unoutweighable (what we may call "black suffering"). And in cases where the sufferers cannot make such evaluations, we may say that suffering at a level of intensity comparable to the suffering deemed unoutweighable by subjects who can make such evaluations should also be considered unoutweighable, and its prevention should be prioritized over all less intense forms of suffering.

Yet this is, of course, all rather theoretical. In practice, even when subjects do have the ability to evaluate their experience, we will, as outside observers, usually not be able to know what their evaluation is — for instance, how someone who is burning alive might evaluate their experience. In practice, all we can do is make informed assessments of what counts as suffering so intense that such an evaluation of unoutweighability would likely be made by the sufferer, assuming an idealized situation where the sufferer is able to evaluate the disvalue of the experience.[122]

---

that their happiness, or other good things about their lives, *can* outweigh the existence of such extreme suffering — i.e. to actively prioritize the evaluations of such notional beings over the evaluations of those enduring, by their own accounts, unoutweighable suffering. What I would consider a profoundly unsympathetic choice.

[122] This once again hints at the point made earlier that we in practice are unable to specify in precise terms 1) what we value in the world, and 2) how to act in accordance with any set of plausible values. Rough, qualified approximations are all we can hope for.

I shall spare the reader from further examples of extreme suffering here in the text, and instead refer to sources, found in the following note, that contain additional cases that are worth considering in order to gain a greater appreciation of extreme suffering and its disvalue.[123] And the crucial question we must ask ourselves in relation to these examples — which, as hinted by the quote above by Knutsson, are probably far from the worst possible manifestations of suffering — is whether the creation of happiness or any other intrinsic good could ever justify the creation, or the failure to prevent, suffering this bad and worse. If not, this implies that our priority should not be to create happiness or other intrinsic goods, but instead to prevent extreme suffering of this kind above anything else, regardless of where in time and space it may risk emerging.

Objections to SIS

Among the objections against this view I can think of, the strongest, at least at first sight, is the sentiment: but what about that which is most precious in your life? What about the person who is most dear to you? If anything stands a chance of outweighing the disvalue of extreme suffering, surely this is it. In more specific terms: does it not seem plausible to claim that, say, saving the most precious person in one's life could be worth an instance of the very worst form of suffering?

Yet one has to be careful about how this question is construed. If what we mean by "saving" is that we save them from extreme suffering, then we are measuring extreme suffering against extreme suffering, and hence we have not pointed to a rival candidate for outweighing the superlative disvalue of extreme suffering. Therefore, if we are to point to such a candidate, "saving" must here mean something that does not itself involve

---

[123] http://reducing-suffering.org/the-horror-of-suffering/

http://reducing-suffering.org/on-the-seriousness-of-suffering/
http://www.simonknutsson.com/the-seriousness-of-suffering-supplement
https://www.youtube.com/watch?v=RyA_eF7W02s&

extreme suffering, and, if we wish to claim that there is something wholly different from the reduction of suffering that can be put on the scale, it should preferably involve no suffering at all. So the choice we should consider is rather one between 1) the mixed bargain of an instance of the very worst form of suffering, i.e. black suffering, and the continued existence of the most precious person one knows, or 2) the painless discontinuation of the existence of this person, yet without any ensuing suffering for others or oneself.

Now, when phrased in this way, choosing 1) may not sound all that bad to us, especially if we do not know the one who will suffer. Yet this would be cheating — nothing but an appeal to our faulty and all too partial moral intuitions. It clearly betrays the principle of impartiality,[124] according to which it should not matter whom the suffering in question is imposed upon; it should be considered equally disvaluable regardless.[125] Thus, we may equivalently phrase the choice above as being between 1) the continued existence of the most precious person one knows of, yet at the price that this being has to experience a state of extreme suffering, a state this person deems so bad that, according to them, it could never be outweighed by any intrinsic good, or 2) the discontinuation of the existence of this being without any ensuing suffering. When phrased in this way, it actually seems clearer to me than ever that 2) is the superior choice, and that we should adopt the principle of sympathy for intense suffering as our highest ethical principle. For how could one possibly justify imposing such extreme, and in the mind of the subject unoutweighable, suffering upon the most precious person one knows, suffering that this person would, at least in that moment, rather die than continue to experience? In this way, for me at least, it is no overstatement

---

[124] Or one could equivalently say that it betrays the core virtue of being consistent, as it amounts to treating/valuing similar beings differently.

[125] I make a more elaborate case for this conclusion in my book *You Are Them*.

to say that this objection against the principle of sympathy for intense suffering, when considered more carefully, actually ends up being one of the strongest cases for it.

Another seemingly compelling objection would be to question whether an arbitrarily long duration of intense, yet, according to the subject, not unoutweighable suffering, i.e. red suffering, is really less bad than even just a split second of suffering that is deemed unoutweighable, i.e. black suffering. Counter-intuitively, my response, at least in this theoretical case, would be to bite the bullet and say "yes". After all, if we take the subject's own reports as the highest arbiter of the (dis)value of experiential states, then the black suffering cannot be outweighed by anything, whereas the red suffering can. Also, it should be noted that this thought experiment likely conflicts with quite a few sensible, real-world intuitions we have. For instance, in the real world, it seems highly likely that a subject who experiences extreme suffering for a long time will eventually find it unbearable, and say that nothing can outweigh it, contrary to the hypothetical case we are considering. Another such confounding real-world intuition might be one that reminds us that most things in the real world tend to fluctuate in some way, and hence, intuitively, it seems like there is a significant risk that a person who endures red suffering for a long time will also experience black suffering (again contrary to the actual conditions of the thought experiment), and perhaps even experience a lot of it, in which case this indeed is worse than a mere split second of black suffering on any account.

Partly for this latter reason, my response would also be different in practice. For again, in the real world, we are never able to determine the full consequences of our actions, and nor are we usually able to determine from the outside whether someone is experiencing red or black suffering, which implies that we have to take uncertainty and risks into account. Also because, even if we did know that a subject deemed some state of suffering as "merely" red at one point, this would not imply that their suffering at other moments where they appear to be in a similar state will also be deemed red as opposed to black. For in the real world it is indeed to be expected that significant fluctuations will occur, as well as that "the same suffering", in one sense at least, will be felt as worse over time. Indeed, if the suffering is extreme, it all but surely will be deemed unbearable eventually.

Thus, in the real world, any large amount of extreme suffering is likely to include black suffering too, and therefore, regardless of whether we think some black suffering is worse than any amount of red suffering, the only reasonable thing to do in practice is to avoid getting near the abyss altogether.

Bias Alert: We Prefer to Not Consider Extreme Suffering

As noted above, merely thinking about extreme suffering can evoke unpleasant feelings that we naturally prefer to avoid. And this is significant for at least two reasons. First, it suggests that thinking deeply about extreme suffering might put our mental health at risk, and hence that we have good reason, and a strong personal incentive, to avoid engaging in such deeper thinking. Second, in part for this first reason, it suggests that we are biased against thinking deeply about extreme suffering, and hence biased against properly appreciating the true horror and disvalue of such suffering. Somewhat paradoxically, (the mere thought of) the horror of extreme suffering keeps us from fully appreciating the true scope of this horror. And this latter consideration is significant in the context of trying to fairly evaluate the plausibility of views that say we should give special priority to such suffering, including the view presented above.

Indeed, one can readily tell a rather plausible story about how many of the well-documented biases we reviewed previously might conspire to produce such a bias against appreciating the horror of suffering.[126] For one, we have wishful thinking, our tendency to believe as true what we wish were true, which in this case likely pulls us toward the belief that it can't b e *that* bad, and that, surely, there must be something of greater value, some grander quest worth pursuing in this world than the mere negative, rather anti-climatic "journey" of alleviating and preventing extreme suffering. Like most inhabitants of Omelas, we wishfully avoid giving much thought to the bad parts, and instead focus on all the good — although our sin is, of course, much greater than theirs, as the bad parts in the real world are indescribably worse on every metric, including total amount, relative proportions, and intensity.

To defend this wishfully established view, we then have our confirmation bias. We comfortably believe that it cannot really be that bad, and so in perfect confirmation bias textbook-style, we shy away from and ignore data that might suggest otherwise. We choose not to look at the horrible real-world examples that might change our minds, and to not think too deeply about the arguments that challenge our merry conceptions of value and ethics. All of this for extremely good reasons, of course. Or at least so we tell ourselves.[127]

---

[126] One might object that it makes little sense to call a failure to appreciate the value of something a bias, as this is a moral rather than an empirical disagreement, to which I would respond: 1) the two are not as easy to separate as is commonly supposed (cf. Putnam, 2002), 2) one clearly can be biased against fairly considering an argument for a moral position — for instance, we can imagine an example where someone encounters a moral position and then, due to being brought up in a culture that dislikes that moral position, fails to properly engage with and understand this position, although this person would in fact agree with it upon reflection; such a failure can fairly be said to be due to bias — and 3) at any rate, the question concerning what it is like to experience certain states of consciousness *is* a factual matter, including how horrible they are deemed from the inside, and this is something we can be factually wrong about as outside observers.

[127] Not that sparing our own mental health is not a good reason for not doing something potentially traumatizing, but the question is just whether it is really worth letting our view of our personal and collective purpose in life be handicapped and biased, at the very least less well-informed than it otherwise could be, for that reason. Whether such self-imposed ignorance can really be justified, both to ourselves and the world at large.

Next, we have groupthink and, more generally, our tendency to conform to our peers. Others do not seem to believe that extreme suffering is *that* horrible, or that reducing it should be our supreme goal, and thus our bias to conform smoothly points us in the same direction as our wishful thinking and confirmation bias. That direction being: "Come on, lighten up! Extreme suffering is probably not *that* bad, and it probably can be outweighed somehow. This is what I want to believe, it is what my own established and comfortable belief says, and it is what virtually all my peers seem to believe. Why in the world, then, would I believe anything else?"

Telling such a story of bias might be considered an unfair move, a crude exercise in pointing fingers at others and exclaiming "You're just biased!", and admittedly it is to some extent. Nonetheless, I think two things are worth noting in response to such a sentiment. First, rather than having its origin in finger pointing at others, the source of this story is really autobiographical: it is a fair characterization of how my own mind managed to repudiate the immense horror and primacy of extreme suffering for a long time. And merely combining this with the belief that I am not a special case then tentatively suggests that a similar story might well apply to the minds of others too.

Second, it should be noted that a similar story cannot readily be told in the opposite direction — about the values defended here. In terms of wishful thinking, it is not particularly wishful or feel-good to say that extreme suffering is immensely bad, and that there is nothing of greater value in the world than to prevent it. That is not a pretty or satisfying story for anyone. The view also seems difficult to explain via an appeal to confirmation bias, since many of those who hold this view of extreme suffering, including myself, did not hold it from the outset, but instead changed their minds toward it upon considering arguments and real-world examples that support it. The same holds true of our tendency to conform to our peers. For although virtually nobody appears to seriously doubt that suffering has disvalue, the view that nothing could be more important than preventing extreme suffering does not seem widely held, much less widely expressed. It lies far from the narrative about the ultimate mission and future purpose of humanity that prevails in most circles, which runs more along the lines of "Surely it must all be worth it somehow, right?"

This last consideration about how we stand in relation to our peers is perhaps especially significant. For the truth is that we are a signalling species: we like to appear cool and impressive.[128] And to express the view that nothing matters more than the prevention of extreme suffering seems a most unpromising way of doing so. It has a strong air of darkness and depression about it, and, worst of all, it is not a signal of strength and success, which is perhaps what we are driven the most to signal to others, prospective friends and mates alike. Such success signalling is not best done with darkness, but with light: by exuding happiness, joy, and positivity. This is the image of ourselves, including our worldview, that we are naturally inclined to project, which then ties into the remark made above — that this view does not seem widely held, "much less widely expressed". For even if we are inclined to hold this view, we appear motivated to not express it, lest we appear like a sad loser.

In sum, by my lights, effective altruism proper is equivalent to effectively reducing extreme suffering. This, I would argue, is the highest meaning of "improving the world" and "benefiting others", and hence what should be considered the ultimate goal of effective altruism. The principle of sympathy for intense suffering argued for here stems neither from depression, nor resentment, nor hatred. Rather, it simply stems, as the

---

[128] Again, Robin Hanson and Kevin Simler's book *The Elephant in the Brain* makes an excellent case for this claim.

name implies, from a deep sympathy for intense suffering.[129] It stems from a firm choice to side with the evaluations of those who are superlatively worst off, and from this choice follows a principled unwillingness to allow the creation of such suffering for the sake of any amount of happiness or any other intrinsic good. And while it is true that this principle has the implication that it would have been better if the world had never existed, I think the fault here is to be found in the world, not the principle.

Most tragically, some pockets of the universe are in a state of insufferable darkness — a state of black suffering. In my view, such suffering is like a black hole that sucks all light out of the world. Or rather: the intrinsic value of all the light of the world pales in comparison to the disvalue of this darkness. Yet, by extension, this also implies that there *is* a form of light whose value *does* compare to this darkness, and that is the kind of light we should aspire to become, namely the light that brightens and prevents this darkness.[130] We shall delve into how this can best be done shortly, but first we shall delve into another issue: our indefensibly anthropocentric take on altruism and "philanthropy".

---

[129] And hence being animated by this principle is perfectly compatible with living a happy, joyous, and meaningful life. Indeed, I would argue that it provides the deepest meaning one could possibly find.

[130] I suspect both the content and phrasing of the last couple of sentences are inspired by the following quote I saw written on Facebook by Robert Daoust: "What is at the center of the universe of ethics, I suggest, is not the sun of the good and its play of bad shadows, but the black hole of suffering."

ANTI-SPECIESISM

"[…] 'speciesism,' by analogy with racism, must also be condemned."[131]
— Peter Singer, *The Effective Altruism Handbook*

Speciesism, as noted earlier, is discrimination against beings based only on their species membership.[132] And if we are to stay true to the core virtue of impartiality, such discrimination must be rejected. Doing so, however, is a demanding challenge, as a rejection of speciesism goes against virtually everything our biology, culture, and rationalizing minds insistently tell us. It requires us to dismantle "common sense" and to dissolve deeply ingrained attitudes. Not least, it requires us to steer clear of the ever-threatening stumbling block that is our comfortable beliefs.

The Indefensibility of Our Prevailing View

The prevailing view of the respective moral status of human and non-human individuals is that the former matter far more than the latter, if the latter indeed matter at all. The question, then, is what reasons can be given for this difference in our view? A common response is that the reason for our discrimination is that humans are more intelligent than other animals.

---

[131] Carey, 2015, p. 98.

[132] Horta, 2010b. Also see http://www.animal-ethics.org/speciesism/

Yet the problem with this claim is that we do not assign differential moral value to human individuals on the basis of their "intelligence", no matter how broadly we construe this term. Humans who do not possess certain cognitive abilities, such as the ability to speak or plan for the future, are not considered less morally valuable than those who do possess them, which forces us to reconsider this purported reason for our discrimination. As Peter Singer notes: "If possessing a higher degree of intelligence does not entitle one human to use another for his or her own ends, how can it entitle humans to exploit nonhumans for the same purpose?"[133]

So if not intelligence, what might then be the reason? If one were to try to be more sophisticated, one might claim that the crucial difference is that humans are more sentient than other animals. Because we have a larger brain, we feel pain and suffering much more intensely than do members of other species, and therefore our discrimination is justified.

Yet the claim that humans are more sentient than other animals is highly dubious. For on what grounds can we assert that, say, a mouse or a fish feels pain any less intensely than a human does? Merely appealing to the fact that they have smaller brains certainly will not do. After all, children have smaller brains than adults, yet should children feel pain any less intensely than adults? It appears they do not, and the opposite could well be the case. The truth is that we have no reason to believe that a larger brain, be it in terms of its number of neurons or in terms of its mass, necessarily gives rise to more intense experiences. Sure, it seems reasonable to expect that there is *some* relationship between brain complexity and the quality and intensity of the experiences a brain can give rise to.[134] Yet this does not imply that bigger brains necessarily give

---

[133] Carey, 2015, p. 98.

[134] Oscar Horta comments (edited slightly):

There's certainly a relationship between brain complexity and the complexity of experiences, but regarding the intensity... It's a common claim, yet it's just a

rise to more intense experiences than smaller brains, just as we cannot say that beings with bigger thighs necessarily run faster than beings with smaller thighs, even though there surely is *some* relationship between thigh size and running ability. Humans, for instance, have larger thighs than domestic cats, but that clearly does not imply that we can outrun them. Similarly, it might well be the case that our larger brains do not mediate more intense experiences than do the brains of, say, domestic cats, or any other animal with the relevant brain structures. Indeed, as Steven Pinker notes, "We have every reason to believe that cats suffer as much as humans do."[135]

Our investigations into the physical signatures of conscious experience indeed give us little reason to believe that the number of neurons found in the brain is of the greatest relevance when it comes to the intensity of its experiences. For instance, we know that more than half the neurons in the human brain are found in the cerebellum, a brain structure that does not seem to play a big role for our conscious experience, if any, while a minority are found in the cerebrum and the limbic system, whose activity most aspects of our conscious experience, if not all, seem to depend upon. Hence, what seems most relevant to the capacity to experience conscious states such as pain and suffering is not the number of neurons found in the brain, but rather certain brain structures, and these structures are found across the vertebrate line, with analogous structures found in many invertebrates.[136] They are anything but uniquely human.

---

supposition. I haven't seen any evidence for it. The intensity of a bad experience is different from how nuanced that experience is.

[135] Quoted from https://www.youtube.com/watch?v=ooTcyioNIZ4

[136] See for instance the so-called Cambridge Declaration on Consciousness, which notes that simple states of consciousness may have arisen long before vertebrate species arose, implying that conscious states may be shared not only by all vertebrates, but also by many invertebrates too. It also states that:

The absence of a neocortex does not appear to preclude an organism from experiencing affective states. Convergent evidence indicates that non-human animals

And not only may other beings feel such experiences as intensely as humans do, they may even experience them more intensely. As David Pearce notes:

> We often find it convenient to act as though the capacity to suffer were somehow inseparably bound up with linguistic ability or ratiocinative prowess. Yet there is absolutely no evidence that this is the case, and a great deal that it isn't. The functional regions of the brain which subserve physical agony, the "pain centres", and the mainly limbic substrates of emotion, appear in phylogenetic terms to be remarkably constant in the vertebrate line. The neural pathways involving serotonin, the periaqua-ductal grey matter, bradykinin, dynorphin, ATP receptors, the major opioid families, substance P, etc. all existed long before hominids walked the earth. Not merely is the biochemistry of suffering disturbingly similar where not effectively type-identical across a wide spectrum of vertebrate (and even some invertebrate) species. It is at least possible that members of any species whose members have more pain cells exhibiting greater synaptic density than humans sometimes suffer more atrociously than we do, whatever their notional "intelligence".[137]

The possibility that beings of other species may experience suffering more intensely than humans has also been raised by zoologist James Serpell,

---

have the neuroanatomical, neurochemical, and neurophysiological substrates of conscious states along with the capacity to exhibit intentional behaviors. Consequently, the weight of evidence indicates that humans are not unique in possessing the neurological substrates that generate consciousness. Non-human animals, including all mammals and birds, and many other beings, including octopuses, also possess these neurological substrates.
http://fcmconference.org/img/CambridgeDeclarationOnConsciousness.pdf

[137] https://www.hedweb.com/hedethic/hedon1.htm#taste

who notes that, unlike other animals, humans can rationalize their pain, which can help reduce it.[138] Richard Dawkins has made an evolutionary argument for the same conclusion:

> [...] I can see a Darwinian reason why there might even be a negative correlation between intellect and susceptibility to pain. [...]
>
> Isn't it plausible that a clever species such as our own might need less pain, precisely because we are capable of intelligently working out what is good for us, and what damaging events we should avoid? Isn't it plausible that an unintelligent species might need a massive wallop of pain, to drive home a lesson that we can learn with less powerful inducement?
>
> At very least, I conclude that we have no general reason to think that non-human animals feel pain less acutely than we do, and we should in any case give them the benefit of the doubt.[139]

But even if we were to grant the dubious assumption that the smaller brains of most non-human animals mediate less intense experiences than do the bigger brains of humans, this would still not justify disregarding them in moral terms. After all, there are also humans who have much smaller brains than most other humans, such as those who are born without cerebral hemispheres.[140] Of course, when it comes to such

---

[138] See about ten minutes into the movie *Speciesism: The Movie*. Serpell's point seems to pertain mainly to the intensity of pain and suffering, yet it is also true of many sources of suffering and distress. For instance, many non-human individuals are scared and distressed by fireworks, whereas humans, due to an understanding that they are not in danger, mostly are not.

[139] Dawkins, 2011. See also "Richard Dawkins: No Civilized Person Accepts Slavery, So Why Do We Accept Animal Cruelty?": https://www.youtube.com/watch?v=_4SnBCPzBl0

[140] For instance, some children with hydranencephaly have no cerebral cortex at all: http://www.ncbi.nlm.nih.gov/pubmed/18435419

humans, it is again clear that the assumption that smaller-brained persons suffer less than bigger-brained ones is highly questionable, and the opposite cannot readily be ruled out — i.e. that they may experience many sensations more intensely than do those with bigger brains. Yet even if we were to accept the claim that such humans suffer less, what would the implications be? Not that significant, it seems, as it is clear that all sentient humans are of intrinsic moral value regardless of how small their brains may be, beings whose suffering we should alleviate, and whose fundamental interests should never be trumped by the trivial interests of others. And, needless to say, the same applies to all sentient beings whose brains are similarly different from the average human brain. To believe otherwise would be to engage in discrimination based on species membership and nothing else, which is exactly what the attempted justification for our speciesism above sought to distance itself from.

More generally, for any cognitive ability we may point to as the crucial ability that non-human animals do not possess, we can point to human individuals who also do not possess this ability. Yet when it comes to such human individuals, very few seem tempted to argue that we are justified in discriminating against them based on such differences. Indeed, we actively deny that this is the case, which suggests that these differences are not the real reason we discriminate against non-human individuals, and that we instead merely invoke these differences as a rationalization.

Indeed, as the above indicates, it is quite clear that the root source of our speciesism is not a careful examination of the neurophysiology of non-human animals, but instead, rather unsurprisingly, something much more crude. For more than anything, our moral intuitions appear animated by a "bodyism" of sorts — an ethic of human bodies in particular. Because, after all, we would never find it justifiable to morally disregard and kill a sentient being with a human body just because this being has the mind of a cow or a chicken, or any other kind of mind. So why, then, do we find it okay to morally disregard and kill a cow or a chicken with reference to the fact that they have the mind of a cow or a chicken? Clearly, the mind is not the determining factor for us. If only we transplanted the mind-brain of any sentient non-human animal into a human body, this would, cf. the observation above, protect this being from our speciesism. And this perfectly exposes our ethical failure on this point, as it obviously betrays one of the most fundamental ethical values we all hold, namely that we should not value a being differently based on the external appearances of that being.

Quite simply, our speciesist attitudes and practices cannot be justified.[141] Discrimination based on species membership is no more justifiable than discrimination against humans based on their race, sex, or cognitive abilities, and it should be condemned just as strongly. Add to this the fact that non-human beings comprise the vast majority of sentient beings on the planet — more than 99.99 percent of sentient vertebrates are non-human[142] — and it suddenly becomes apparent just how extraordinarily skewed and indefensible our prevailing moral and altruistic focus is. Indeed, it is difficult to overstate just how biased and ineffective our altruistic efforts are bound to be as long as we fail to go beyond our speciesism — as long as we leave out more than 99.99 percent of sentient individuals in virtually all our moral deliberations and altruistic endeavors. By analogy, imagine the value and efficacy of an altruistic focus that pertains exclusively to people of Scandinavian descent as opposed to all of humanity; hardly the ideal focus to adopt in order to help as many beings as possible. And yet this analogy fails to compare even remotely to the current ratio of the number of beings we are concerned with to the number of beings we should be concerned with.

---

[141] For a more elaborate case for this conclusion, see Horta 2010b and *Speciesism: Why It Is Wrong and the Implications of Rejecting It.*

[142] http://reducing-suffering.org/how-many-wild-animals-are-there/

Our offended anthropocentric minds will, of course, be most eager to object here, with anything that might have a remote chance of bringing us back to a familiar equilibrium of comforting beliefs. It might object that, "If you count the total number of brain cells found in different classes of animals, our focus is actually not skewed". Yet this is wrong, since there are more than a hundred times as many neurons in the total mass of insect brains as there are in all human brains.[143] Thus, human neurons in fact comprise less than one percent of all neurons on the planet. Try another strategy, then: "We should factor in brain-to-body ratio too". Yet this only favors insects even more, as they generally have large such ratios, much larger than humans. Small ants, for example, have a brain-to-body mass ratio of 1:7, while it lies around 1:40 in humans.[144]

However much we may try, there is just no way to avoid the conclusion that our prevailing altruistic and moral focus is indefensibly narrow. And as long as that remains true, as long as virtually all of our altruistic attention is devoted to much less than 0.01 percent of the sentient beings on the planet, our attempts at being *effectively* altruistic are bound to be a complete failure.

---

[143] Assuming there are 10 billion humans on the planet with 100 billion neurons each, this gives a total human neuron count of 10^{21} (which is, of course, an overestimate), whereas it is estimated that there are 10^{18} insects (that is a conservative estimate; some estimates are a full order of magnitude higher), and making the assumption that they have 10^{5} neurons on average (although fruit flies and ants have 2.5 times as many, bees and cockroaches ten times as many), this yields a total number of 10^{23}. The total neuron count of fish also dominates that of humans by a full order of magnitude on the plausible estimate that there are 10^{15} fish with 10^{7} neurons each on average (the neuron count of an adult zebrafish), which yields a total of 10^{22} fish neurons. Also see https://eukaryotewritesblog.com/how-many-neurons-are-there/

[144] As for whether insects feel pain, see the following essays:

http://reducing-suffering.org/do-bugs-feel-pain/
http://reducing-suffering.org/the-importance-of-insect-suffering/

The Implications of Rejecting Speciesism

The main implications of rejecting speciesism are quite straightforward, if difficult to come to terms with for minds as anthropocentrically built and schooled as ours. One implication is that we should stop imposing gratuitous suffering on any sentient being. In particular, we should abolish the property status of non-human individuals and end our practice of eating and otherwise frivolously exploiting them. For just as a rejection of racism is not compatible with keeping individuals belonging to another race — or indeed any human individual — as property, much less eating and otherwise exploiting their body parts, a rejection of speciesism is not compatible with commodifying, eating, and frivolously exploiting individuals belonging to another species. The prevailing idea that we all prefer to nod along with on this matter holds something else, of course, namely that we should just focus on "treating them better". Yet this is not a position we would ever advocate or accept in relation to human beings, or indeed any notional sentient individual with a human body. And neither can we defend doing so merely because the sentient beings in question have non-human bodies.[145]

We are indeed far detached from our own core principles on this inconvenient issue. For not only are we discriminating against beings based on their external appearances, we also fail to stay true to the concern for suffering that we claim to have. For instance, many people say that they will not accept the imposition of torture on any individual for any reason, least of all for the sake of pleasure. And yet the dietary choices of virtually all of us fly directly in the face of this claim. Consider, for instance, how a cow exploited by the dairy industry is treated. Such a cow is impregnated via forced insemination so as to make her lactate, and

---

[145] Elaborate arguments for these claims are found in *Why We Should Go Vegan; Why "Happy Meat" Is Always Wrong*; and *Speciesism: Why It Is Wrong and The Implications of Rejecting It.*

when she eventually gives birth, her baby is stolen away from her. And this happens throughout her life. A continuous cycle of forced pregnancy followed by the stealing of her babies. If this were done to a human, we would not hesitate to call it what it is: torture. Yet most of us routinely throw our money after an industry that does exactly this, not to one being, but to tens of millions of beings every year, and for no higher reason than our own pleasure and convenience. And this is not only true of dairy, but of all our exploitation of non-human animals. In the egg industry, for example, male chicks are routinely ground up while alive,[146] and the ways in which we slaughter other beings for their flesh also lead to torturous suffering in innumerable cases. For example, in the United States alone, a million birds are boiled alive every year by mistake.[147] And at least as brutal is our killing of fish, the vertebrates we kill in the greatest numbers by far, usually without even the pretense of doing it "humanely" — they are torn out of the ocean, suffocated, and decapitated without regard for the extreme pain and suffering this causes.[148]

Our actions are nothing less than perfectly inconsistent with our proclaimed opposition to torture and torturous suffering. Contra high-minded ideals of walking away from Omelas, we find ourselves actively walking right into the opposite scenario, a world in which countless beings live like the miserable child in the basement in Omelas — compare that child's life with the average life on a "factory farm" — and in which many of these beings are routinely subjected to horrors that are far worse still. All for the sake of the pleasure and convenience of a tiny minority of beings on the planet. This is indeed much worse than an inverse Omelas

---

[146] See for instance https://www.youtube.com/watch?v=GN5H9audCRQ

[147] http://nation.time.com/2013/10/29/nearly-one-million-chickens-and-turkeys-unintentionally-boiled-alive-each-year-in-u-s/

[148] As for the idea that fish do not feel pain, see https://www.smithsonianmag.com/science-nature/fish-feel-pain-180967764/

scenario. Yet as George Bernard Shaw observed, custom will reconcile people to any atrocity.

Wild Animal Suffering

Ceasing to actively harm non-human animals for morally frivolous reasons is far from the only thing that follows from a rejection of speciesism, however. We must also start helping them. For the vast majority of sentient beings on the planet, and hence the vast majority of suffering by virtually any measure, is found not in farms, but in the wild.[149] In terms of presently existing beings, this is where the greatest scope for altruism is found.

To most, this probably seems like an absurd claim. After all, 1) aren't non-human animals in nature mostly well off? and 2) why should we feel obliged to help them rather than just let them be? The former sentiment reflects a common idyllic view of nature, a view that is sadly wrong.[150] For as Peter Singer notes: "Evolution is an impersonal natural process that has no regard for the wellbeing of the individual creatures it has produced."[151] And the reality of life in the wild reflects this fact all too well: it is a condition of abject poverty.

Just like humans who live in extreme poverty, non-human beings in nature suffer from readily preventable diseases, starvation, parasitism, lack of basic safety, etc. — and many of them are eaten alive.[152] And just like

---

[149] http://reducing-suffering.org/how-many-wild-animals-are-there/

[150] See for instance Faria & Paez, 2015, as well as Oscar Horta's essay "Debunking the Idyllic View of Natural Processes":
https://masalladelaespecie.files.wordpress.com/2012/05/debunkingidyllicviewhorta.pdf

[151] https://www.project-syndicate.org/commentary/are-insects-conscious-by-peter-singer-2016-05?barrier=accessreg

[152] http://www.utilitarian-essays.com/suffering-nature.html
http://reducing-suffering.org/wp-content/uploads/2014/10/wild-animals.pdf
Also see the talk: "Reducing Wild Animal Suffering":

humans, non-human individuals have an interest in avoiding such misery, which leads us to the second question — why should we care and do something about it? The simple answer is: because not considering the interests of these beings would be an indefensible, speciesist position. When it comes to humans, we realize that we should do something to alleviate conditions of abject poverty and extreme misery, even if we have played no part in bringing them about. And to think that this changes when the afflicted beings are non-human individuals is merely to entertain unjustified discrimination. It is to fail to give proper consideration to the interests of beings merely because they belong to another species. [153]

"But", one may object, "what can we do about such suffering?" This is no doubt a difficult question to answer in much detail at this early stage where very few people have explored it seriously. Some answers have been proposed, however, one of them being the practice of "compassionate biology" defended by David Pearce, which entails cross-species fertility-regulation via immunocontraception and the use of CRISPR-based gene drives, as well as other technological means, to create "a pan-species welfare state in tomorrow's Nature reserves: in short, "high-tech Jainism"."[154]

Yet even if we had no proposed answers of this sort, we would not have reason to dismiss the issue altogether. Again, consider the case of human poverty: the mere fact that this is a difficult problem to solve does not mean that we should give up and do nothing. On the contrary, it implies that we should do more research and think harder about how we might be able to improve the situation. So too with the problem of suffering in the wild: its tractability appears rather uncertain at this point,

---

https://www.youtube.com/watch?v=4aa6g1y4l8I

[153] For an essay on why most people do not seem to care about wild animal suffering, see Ben Davidow's essay "Why Most People Don't Care About Wild Animal Suffering": http://reducing-suffering.org/why-most-people-dont-care-about-wild-animal-suffering/

[154] https://www.gene-drives.com/

which suggests that, rather than ignore it or give up, we should do more research, as done by the organization Wild Animal Suffering Research.[155] Supporting such research efforts is one thing we can do at this point. Another is to promote the idea that we should do something about the problem of suffering in nature, and to promote concern for non-human individuals in general, both of which are the focus of the organization Animal Ethics. Thus, the idea that there is nothing we can do about this problem at this point is really quite false.[156]

Bias Alert: We Should Expect to Be Extremely Biased

Our speciesist bias has already been alluded to in an earlier chapter, yet it is still worth delving deeper into it here. For if ever there were a bias we evolved to fail to transcend, it is surely this. Think about it: we evolved in a context in which our survival depended on our killing and eating non-human individuals. For our entire evolutionary history, the questioning of such a practice, and the belief that non-human individuals should be taken seriously in moral terms, meant a radically decreased probability of continued survival. And this would also apply to one's entire tribe if one were to start spreading such a sentiment, which may well explain the visceral disgust and acute threat that many of us can readily feel upon engaging with supporters of this sentiment today. In other words, having significant moral concern for non-human individuals was not a recipe for survival in our evolutionary history. It was a death sentence. For this reason alone, we should expect to be *extremely* biased on this matter.

And yet this evolutionary tale actually falls rather short of being the full story, as there is also a cultural story to tell, and at this level we find

---

155 https://was-research.org/

Also see Michael Dickens's essay "The Myth that Reducing Wild Animal Suffering Is Intractable":
http://mdickens.me/2016/04/22/the_myth_that_reducing_wild_animal_suffering_is_intractable/

156 http://www.animal-ethics.org/working-for-a-future-with-fewer-harms-to-wild-animals/

even more reasons to expect our outlook to be intensely biased. For on top of our speciesist biological hardware, we also have the software of cultural programming running, and what it runs is the ultimate propaganda campaign against concern for non-human individuals. Indeed, if we ran just a remotely similar campaign toward humans, we would consider the term "propaganda" a gross understatement. Their body parts are for sale at every supermarket and on the menu for virtually every meal; their skin is ripped off their bodies and used for handbags, shoes, and sports equipment; their names used pejoratively in every other sentence. Why, indeed, would anyone expect this to leave our moral cognition with respect to these beings biased in the least? Or rather, why should we expect to stand *any* chance whatsoever of having just a single rational thought about the moral status of these beings and our obligations toward them? Well, we shouldn't. Not without immense amounts of effort spent rebelling against our crude nature and the atrocious culture it has spawned.

Another bias that is relevant to consider, on top of these considerations, is that human altruism tends to be motivated by a hidden drive to show others how likable we are, and to increase our own social status.[157] To think that we transcend this motive merely by calling ourselves "effective" altruists would be naive. The problem, then, is that rejecting speciesism and taking the implications of such a rejection seriously is, sadly, extremely uncool. If one were to do so, one would become more than a little obnoxious and unlikeable in the eyes of most people, more like a favorite object of ridicule than of admiration, which is not enticing for social creatures like us. So even if reason unanonymously says that we should reject speciesism, we have a thousand and one social reasons that say just the opposite.

As mentioned earlier, there are also psychological studies that demonstrate the existence of strong biases in our view of non-human

---

[157] This claim is argued for at length in Hanson and Simler's *The Elephant in the Brain*.

individuals, such as that we "value individuals of certain species less than others even when beliefs about intelligence and sentience are accounted for".[158] And we also diminish and deny the mental capacities of the kinds of beings whom we consider food — a denial that is increased by "expectations regarding the immediate consumption" of such beings.[159] These forms of bias should give us pause and cause us to entertain some serious self-examination. Yet, sadly, what most of us do instead is to simply ignore it. Suddenly, debiasing has never seemed so uncool and unvirtuous for some strange reason.

Indeed, even in the effective altruism movement, this most inconvenient and uncool issue tends to be ignored with great skill, which unfortunately renders this movement — at least in practice, at the present moment — mostly a movement of Effective Anthropocentrism, despite its own stated ideals to be something more.[160] Consider, for example, charity evaluators like GiveWell and Giving What We Can, which evaluate charities based purely on their impact on human beings. It is difficult to see how such an evaluation process is consistent with a rejection of speciesism, any more than a rejection of racism is consistent with charity evaluation that focuses only on charities' impact on white people's lives

---

[158] Caviola et al, 2018.

[159] Bastian et al, 2012.

[160] For example, a recent survey of self-identified effective altruists found that a great plurality of respondents, almost 41 percent, found human poverty to be the most important cause, while only around ten percent considered "animal welfare" the most important cause (cf. http://effective-altruism.com/ea/1e5/ea_survey_2017_series_cause_area_preferences/), which is difficult to reconcile with 1) the fact that a condition of abject poverty affects at least a million times more non-human beings in the wild than it does humans; recall our scope neglect and speciesist bias here (and this number is indeed only considering vertebrates), 2) the fact that human poverty is far from being as neglected as the plight of non-human individuals on a global scale, and 3) the fact that human poverty is declining rapidly (https://ourworldindata.org/extreme-poverty#extreme-poverty-in-a-historical-perspective), while the number of non-human beings made to suffer on factory farms and killed by humanity on a global scale is increasing rapidly (http://www.wri.org/sites/default/files/uploads/fish_0.jpg ; https://commons.wikimedia.org/wiki/File:Global-meat-consumption-1961-2009.png).

and well-being when other groups are also impacted.[161] These charity evaluators do not hesitate to accept the conclusion that money can save more lives in poorer countries, and to boldly state and act on this conclusion. Yet when it comes to the possibility that money may save more lives if we spend it on helping individuals who belong to another species — perhaps 13,000 times as many, cf. the chapter on monetary donation[162] — it seems that little attention is given. And detailed explanations of why this is so are absent, which is strange given the overwhelming numbers (yet perhaps not that strange considering our scope neglect) and the powerful arguments against speciesism,[163] arguments that suggest that it is as wrong as racism.[164] The effective altruism movement is a movement of people who laudably systematize their empathy, yet this empathy is unfortunately, and most indefensibly, mostly confined to a narrow anthropocentric cage.

---

[161] For analyses and evaluations of various actions that do seek to include impacts on non-human individuals, see Brian Tomasik's essays on reducing suffering at http://reducing-suffering.org/

[162] One may object that "saving a life" here means two very different things that are not easy to compare, namely preventing a premature death versus preventing a life on a factory farm. And while this is true, it should be noted that there are many views of value and ethics according to which, other things being equal, the latter is (most likely) better than the former, cf. Bertrand, 2016, as well as the values defended in this book, according to which the highest meaning of "saving a life" is to spare it from suffering, particularly extreme suffering.

[163] Yet perhaps not in light of the considerations and studies cited above, all of which suggest that we should expect to have overwhelming bias and resistance against such arguments, however sound they may be. And also if we consider what direction other well-documented biases, such as wishful thinking and confirmation bias, might steer us toward.

[164] And the bar for making a sound defense for this total neglect of non-human individuals is made high not only by these numbers and these arguments (again, for those arguments, see *Speciesism: Why It Is Wrong and the Implications of Rejecting It*), but also by the preceding considerations that suggest that we all but certainly come from a position of intense bias, something that nobody is exempt from, as we all share human nature as well as an upbringing in a speciesist society. And we shall see additional reasons that raise the bar even higher still in the following chapter, reasons pertaining to the far future, which are arguably the most important ones by far.

In light of the considerations of bias above, however, this is not surprising. In fact, it is exactly what one would expect from *any* movement run by humans, and especially one emerging within our current society which so powerfully reinforces and exaggerates our speciesist dispositions — a society that renders the effective altruism movement a paragon of anti-speciesism by comparison. In actuality, however, it is far from being that. For although anti-speciesism follows directly from the stated core values of the effective altruism movement, this does not imply that it is reflected in the broader movement's actual ground-level convictions and practices, as it indeed is not. The first step forward, then, the first step toward being in better alignment with the stated effective altruist ideals and less ruled by the thick cloud of bias we were born to have on this issue, is to admit this much. To admit that we are extremely biased and to commit to doing better.

FUTURE DIRECTIONS

"We have enormous opportunity to reduce suffering on behalf of sentient creatures."

— Brian Tomasik[165]

So far we have seen a general introduction to some of the main ideas associated with effective altruism, an introduction that concluded on the note that the long-term future seems the most important thing to try to influence from an altruistic perspective, as opposed to focusing exclusively on the next couple of decades that tend to steal all our attention. This was then followed by some arguments for suffering-focused ethics in general, and by a case for the principle of sympathy for intense suffering in particular. Finally, our anthropocentric betrayal of the principle of impartiality was criticized, and indeed our entire approach to altruism deemed fundamentally flawed.

The question is then: given all of this, what are the implications? How do we best help others? Or to phrase this question in more specific terms in accordance with the values I have argued for: how can we best reduce extreme suffering in the future?

And the first thing we should remind ourselves upon considering this question is, once again, that it is an open question. As noted in the chapter

---

[165] https://foundational-research.org/against-wishful-thinking/

on the cruciality of values, even if we had perfect clarity about values, a great amount of empirical uncertainty concerning how we can best act in accordance with those values remains inevitable. All we should expect are highly uncertain answers, at best of a modestly qualified kind. With this in mind, let us see what kind of uncertain, yet modestly qualified answers we can give.

Avoid Trying to Destroy the World

Perhaps the first thing to address is that aiming to destroy the world, what is often claimed to be the main practical implication of the values advocated here, is a highly unlikely candidate for the best thing we can do, and for various reasons.[166] For one, it is conceivable that the best way to reduce extreme suffering is to sustain rather than destroy human civilization, and it must indeed be admitted that there is considerable uncertainty as to whether this is the case.[167]

---

[166] Given our inevitable empirical uncertainty, one can, of course, only express this in terms of probabilities, which means that we admittedly should maintain some non-zero probability in the claim that trying to destroy the world is the best we can do. However, it should be noted that this applies to all plausible consequentialist views — that is, that there is some probability that it would be better to try to destroy the world on all such views, as there is a risk that the future might be very bad otherwise. So in this way, with respect to this question, suffering-focused consequentialist views of the kind advocated here are actually not qualitatively different from other consequentialist views. All that differs between them on this particular question is the exact credence assigned to the claim that we should try to destroy the world, and even here it is not obvious that the respective credences that would be assigned from the perspective of different views are necessarily that different, cf. the sources cited in the following note, as well as the considerations that follow in the text.

[167] For some considerations relevant to this question, see for instance Vinding, 2015b as well as the following:
https://foundational-research.org/risks-of-astronomical-future-suffering/#What_if_human_colonization_is_more_humane_than_ET_colonization
http://www.simonknutsson.com/the-world-destruction-argument/#Is_Killing_Everyone_More_Likely_to_Become_Optimal_from_a_Negative_or_a_Traditional_Utilitarian_Perspective

Yet even if one considers this a most unlikely prospect, there still remain many other reasons not to aim to destroy the world, one being that any specific attempt to destroy the world may well increase extreme suffering in expectation rather than reduce it, as such attempts generally seem most likely to not destroy the world, but to instead have the effect of decreasing stability and cooperation in our future civilization, as well as to decrease compassionate values and concern for suffering. And even if one believed that such attempts in fact do reduce extreme suffering in expectation, it still seems likely that there are other courses of action whose expected value is much greater and which seem more robustly positive.[168] What might those be?

Promoting Deeper Concern for Suffering

One endeavor that seems particularly promising, and which I have attempted to pursue in this book, is that of promoting a deeper conversation about values, especially with an emphasis on the moral significance of extreme suffering, as well as on the moral urgency of preventing suffering versus creating happiness. For it seems likely that the change in values toward greater concern for extreme suffering that could be furthered via such a conversation is among the changes we can make that best reduce extreme suffering. The main reason being, in short, that our values arguably comprise the chief driver of our actions, or at least the greatest driver we can most readily influence, which renders changes in values among the most consequential changes we can make.[169]

---

[168] Again, a similar conclusion may also be defended from the perspective of non-negative ethical views. That is, that extinction may be positive in expectation, yet that there are other actions than trying to directly impact the probability of extinction that seem better in expectation, such as trying to improve the quality of the future.

[169] Some people view moral arguments and advocacy as uncooperative and zero-sum, a view that I reject completely. One can say that it ultimately depends on our conception of reason, and the conception I would defend maintains that there indeed is such a thing as having more or less well-considered, more or less plausible, views of what is valuable (e.g. that a precept like

Among the people who share the view that this is a promising strategy are Brian Tomasik, who has presented a case for why "[...] arguing for suffering-focused ethical principles seems to be a robust and effective advocacy strategy" in his essay "Reasons to Promote Suffering-Focused Ethics",[170] and Simon Knutsson, who has made questions concerning fundamental values, and suffering-focused ethics in particular, the main focus of his work.[171] As for how such deeper reflection and concern pertaining to extreme suffering can best be fostered, it seems promising to formulate and spread clear presentations of arguments in favor of suffering-focused ethics, as well as to familiarize people with some of the unimaginably horrible real-life cases of extreme suffering. A few examples of resources that do one or both of these can be found in the following note.[172]

"maximize suffering" *truly* is less plausible and reasonable than, say, "minimize suffering"; for a more elaborate argument for this particular claim, see the second part of *You Are Them*). More plausible, that is, to our faculties of reason. Or phrased in more operational terms: we may define "most reasonable" or "most plausible" as that which seems most reasonable to our minds all arguments and experiences considered. One may, of course, dispute that we can all converge on the same conclusions on all questions pertaining to values via such reasoning, and there is indeed no doubt that we cannot, at least in practice. Yet it seems equally wrong to claim that the degree of convergence via collective reflection would be zero, and to the extent that such reflection leads us to (at least some) novel views that we all agree are superior to our previous ones, those views are, on my account of reason, indeed truly superior. In that case we have gained (in wisdom, we may call it) in a very real sense; we have not been gamed or "zero-summed".

[170] http://reducing-suffering.org/the-case-for-promoting-suffering-focused-ethics/

[171] As he introduces his own work:

When we try to do something for the world, what should our priorities be? Which values should we have? Most of my research deals with these questions. My take so far is that we should be antispeciesist and focus on reducing extreme suffering. I've worked especially on suffering-focused ethics, which is an umbrella term for moral views that, in practice, favor a focus on reducing suffering.
http://www.simonknutsson.com/

[172] https://foundational-research.org/the-case-for-suffering-focused-ethics/

http://reducing-suffering.org/the-horror-of-suffering/
https://www.youtube.com/watch?v=RyA_eF7W02s ("Preventing Extreme Suffering Has Moral Priority")

To get a clearer sense of why such a focus on values is important, and how different the practical implications of different values can be, consider the practical implications of the following two moral principles: 1) we will not allow the creation of a single instance of the worst forms of suffering (black suffering) for any amount of happiness, and 2) we will allow one day of such suffering for ten years of the most sublime happiness. What kind of future would we accept with these respective principles? Imagine a future in which we colonize space and maximize the number of sentient beings that the accessible universe can sustain over the entire course of the future, which is probably more than 10^{30}.[173] Given this number of beings, and assuming these beings each live a hundred years, principle 2) above would appear to permit a space colonization that all in all creates more than 10^{28} years of black suffering, provided that the other states of experience are sublimely happy. This is how extreme the difference can be between principles like 1) and 2); between whether we consider suffering irredeemable or not. And notice that even if we altered the exchange rate by orders of magnitude — say, by requiring 10^{15} times more sublime happiness per unit of extreme suffering than we did in principle 2) above — we would still allow an enormous amount of extreme suffering to be created; in the concrete case of requiring 10^{15} times more happiness, we would allow more than 10,000 billion years of black suffering.[174]

---

[173] Indeed, Nick Bostrom puts the "lower bound of the number of biological human life-years in the future accessible universe" at 10^{34}, cf. Bostrom, 2013, p. 18, and in his book *Superintelligence*, he estimates that, given that human consciousness can be emulated in different substrates, the accessible universe could sustain 10^{60} such life-years, cf. Bostrom 2014, p. 103.

[174] This way of thinking about the future may also suggest another way of defending not creating so much suffering, for instance in the form of a principle that puts a threshold at a certain amount of such extreme suffering — 10,000 years of it in total, say — above which we will not allow more such suffering for any price. According to such a view, one might then be able to defend continuing life on Earth, while opposing that we spread it elsewhere. Alternatively, one could simply adopt this conclusion as a core ethical principle: that we can

Thus, whether we consider black suffering irredeemable or whether we consider it able to be outweighed by an enormous amount of happiness can clearly have significant practical implications. In terms of the amount of suffering that will exist, it can mean the difference between no suffering and aeons of the worst forms of suffering, and that is how important it is that we think carefully about whether we accept an exchange rate like the one above, or whether we instead think that the absolute amount of such extreme suffering is what matters first and foremost. I have argued that we should favor the latter.[175]

And this actually appears to be a common view, perhaps even the prevailing one, as it seems that minimizing future suffering is also the goal most favored by people in the broader population. At least that is what a survey of 14,866 people, conducted by the Future of Life Institute, indicates.[176] From a list of suggested goals that should be strived for by a future civilization, a clear plurality, comprised by a third of the respondents, favored minimizing suffering. By comparison, significantly fewer, around a fourth, favored maximizing positive experiences. More than that, the survey also found that the vast majority, around 90 percent, wanted life to spread into space, which raises questions about how the many people who favor minimizing suffering would reconcile and weigh these two goals, i.e. spreading life into space and minimizing suffering, to the extent that they are in conflict, which they likely will be.

---

continue life on Earth, yet that we should not create any suffering beyond Earth, no matter how much pleasure or other good things may be gained from it, analogously to how anti-natalists defend continuing existing lives, while opposing the creation of new ones.

[175] The preceding considerations are similar to, and probably in large part inspired by, those found in Brian Tomasik's essays "Omelas and Space Colonization":
http://reducing-suffering.org/omelas-and-space-colonization/
See also his essay "Risks of Astronomical Future Suffering":
https://foundational-research.org/risks-of-astronomical-future-suffering/

[176] https://futureoflife.org/superintelligence-survey/

Yet it is worth noting that, in relation to space colonization, one can argue that it is not even necessary to accept a principle like 1) above, or indeed any remotely suffering-focused view, in order to maintain that we should not spread life beyond Earth, at least not in a condition that is anything like the current one on Earth. This holds true for two reasons we have already visited. The first reason is that, as argued in the chapter on suffering-focused ethics, even on a view according to which we are willing to really push it and endure an unreasonable amount of suffering to gain happiness, the vast majority of moral weight still appears to lie in preventing suffering, at least in terms of the extremes of the potential states of happiness and suffering. On top of that, we have the second reason, namely that the actual state of the world reflects this underlying asymmetric potential all too well in that it, as argued in the chapter on anti-speciesism, sadly most of all resembles an inverse Omelas scenario. A scenario where countless beings are subjected to suffering, often extreme, for the sake of the frivolous pleasure and convenience of a small minority. To spread such a condition would hardly be a defensible use of extraterrestrial matter and energy on any but the most barbaric of views. This condition is not, presumably, the kind of condition most people would want to see spreading into space. Or at least so one hopes.

Minimizing S-Risks

The preceding discussion brings us to another strategy: minimizing risks of astronomical future suffering, sometimes referred to as "s-risks".[177] For as much as we may hope that catastrophic outcomes in which suffering occurs at an astronomical scale will never materialize, the inconvenient truth is that there is a risk they might. And given that the stakes are so

---

[177] https://foundational-research.org/reducing-risks-of-astronomical-suffering-a-neglected-priority/
http://s-risks.org/

high, even a small probability of the realization of such outcomes implies that trying to prevent them can have a large expected value.

It can be difficult to see the relevance of this. After all, how could things possibly turn out so badly? Yet one can say a few things in response to such a sentiment. First, as we saw above, a future that contains suffering on an astronomical scale, and in unacceptable proportions by any reasonable standard, would actually not require anything more radical than that we spread our current sentient condition beyond Earth. Second, the probability of a very bad outcome need only be small for the expected value of trying to prevent it to be high, which implies that, even if we cannot readily envision such an outcome, it is still worth exploring how such an outcome might come about. Third, we know that we have a tendency toward wishful thinking, which should make us highly skeptical of our inclination to dismiss these risks of bad outcomes, especially in light of the two preceding considerations.[178]

Beyond that, the influence of wishful thinking on our assessments of such risks also suggests that a subscription to suffering-focused ethics is not required for a focus on s-risks to make sense. For no matter what kind of trade-off between happiness and suffering, or between other kinds of goods and bads we may find acceptable, there is a real risk that the future will sorely disappoint. And given our propensity for wishful thinking, as well as our propensity to focus on cool and positive things, it seems likely that a focus on such risks generally is, and will remain, neglected on virtually all value systems, which suggests that working to explore and prevent very bad outcomes is of great value — on virtually all value systems. Thus, focusing on improving the quality of the future,[179] particularly by working to avoid very bad outcomes, is plausibly a robust strategy across a wide range of values, not merely suffering-focused ones.

---

[178] See also https://foundational-research.org/against-wishful-thinking/

[179] Cf. http://effective-altruism.com/ea/t3/some_considerations_for_different_ways_to_reduce/

So how may we best prevent s-risks? Some believe the optimal way is to influence the development of emerging technologies, especially artificial intelligence.[180] Other promising strategies include the one outlined above, promoting deeper concern for suffering, as well as the one described in the following section: expanding our moral circle.

Expanding Our Moral Circle

Another endeavor that seems particularly promising for reducing future suffering is to expand our circle of moral consideration. Indeed, it seems that increased concern for suffering and moral circle expansion are both necessary yet insufficient for effectively reducing future suffering. For if we only expand our moral circle, yet fail to deepen our concern for extreme suffering, we will not reduce the risk of scenarios of the kind outlined above, with astronomical levels of extreme suffering allowed for beings within our moral circle in order to bring about large amounts of happiness. At the same time, if we only deepen our concern for suffering without also expanding our moral circle, such deepened concern may end up not encompassing all beings who indeed can suffer, just like many people who care deeply about suffering today work almost exclusively on alleviating human suffering. And as a result, this deepened concern risks failing to pertain to and prevent the vast majority of expected future suffering, and can thereby also permit the creation of astronomical future suffering, although in a different way. Thus, expanding our moral circle is imperative as well.

One way to see its relevance is to consider our current situation in which humanity devotes almost all its altruistic resources and moral attention to a tiny fraction of sentient beings on the planet, while

---

[180] For a case for focusing on artificial intelligence in order to reduce s-risks and bad future outcomes more generally, see
https://foundational-research.org/cause-prioritization-downside-focused-value-systems/

neglecting, and in many cases actively creating, the suffering of the rest. One may, of course, argue that this neglect is unlikely to remain in the future, yet it is not obvious that such a claim is warranted. After all, why would a self-serving bias not persist in powerful agents in the future? And even if confidence in the aforementioned claim is warranted, i.e. even if we are more likely than not to include all sentient beings in our moral circle in the future, there is still a significant risk that we will not, and it seems worth reducing that risk as much as possible given the enormous stakes.

It may also be objected that it is far from clear that there will be any non-human animals in the long-term future, and hence that efforts to expand the moral circle will be in vain. Yet while the former may well be true, the latter does not follow, since 1) there still remains a significant probability that there will be such beings in large numbers in the future (e.g. if conservationism prevails), and 2) it may be that other kinds of vulnerable non-human beings will emerge in the future, such as humanly created non-biological beings. And not only might such beings eventually outnumber humans as much as non-human animals do today, but they may even come to outnumber them by orders of magnitude more. And given that this is perhaps one of the most plausible ways in which an outcome with astronomical amounts of extreme suffering might be realized,[181] it seems that working to expand the moral circle of the future might indeed be one of the most promising ways to reduce s-risks, as well as future suffering more generally.[182] Furthermore, one can also argue that, even if humans or other kinds of similarly powerful agents indeed will comprise the majority of beings in the future, it may still be that the promotion of

---

[181] Cf. https://foundational-research.org/risks-of-astronomical-future-suffering/

[182] See also the following pieces which argue for a similar conclusion:

http://effective-altruism.com/ea/1l0/why_i_prioritize_moral_circle_expansion_over/
http://mdickens.me/2016/09/10/why_im_prioritizing_animal_advocacy/
https://www.slideshare.net/Adriano_Mannino/affecting-the-far-future-with-the-animal-cause

concern for comparatively vulnerable beings is the best way to reduce future suffering, as the powerful beings of the future likely will be better able to help themselves than we are today, whereas we might well be able to influence how much consideration such agents will devote to the vulnerable beings whom they can impact. And again, it should be noted that moral circle expansion is a robust, high-value strategy from a wide variety of value systems, not merely suffering-focused ones.

How the moral circle of the future can best be expanded stands very much as an open question, and it is indeed this very question that the organization Sentience Institute seeks to explore (cf. the chapter on monetary donation). Yet it seems that the promotion of concern for the morally excluded non-human beings who currently exist is a good place to start, whether done by exposing people to the extensive cruelty that is inflicted upon them, or by presenting arguments of a more abstract nature, such as those against speciesism.[183] Such increased concern would not only reduce a lot of suffering in the short term, but would also, arguably even more importantly, help us think more clearly in moral terms. That is, it would help move us toward a moral outlook less blinded by indefensible anthropocentrism. An outlook that in turn likely helps us see the importance of future concern for vulnerable minds, and of creating a future with less suffering for them.

Researching and Reflecting on the Question

The question of how we can best reduce the amount of extreme suffering that will occur in the future is not merely open, but also highly neglected, which makes additional research on it seem of great value. And there are indeed many diverse questions that are relevant to explore in this context, from how a deeper appreciation of extreme suffering can best be

---

[183] Cf. https://sentience-politics.org/animal-advocates-focus-antispeciesism-not-veganism/

promoted, to what the physical signatures of suffering are, i.e. what the place of suffering is in the world. These questions matter deeply for our endeavor to reduce suffering, as the sophistication of our answers to them largely determines how effectively we can pursue it.

For instance, take the question of what the physical signatures of suffering are. How can we effectively reduce suffering if we do not have at least a decent answer to this question? It seems that we cannot, and even relatively small changes in our answer to this question can imply enormous differences in terms of practical implications. Such differences in views of the nature of suffering are also, to take a concrete example, partly what explain the differences between the approach to reducing suffering pursued by David Pearce, who advocates the abolition of suffering via biotechnology,[184] and that pursued by Brian Tomasik and the researchers at the Foundational Research Institute, who view suffering in more abstract (as opposed to concrete) terms, and who expect almost all future suffering to be digital rather than biological.[185]

This difference has wide-ranging implications, both for short-term and long-term efforts to reduce suffering. For instance, if David Pearce is right in believing that suffering can be abolished in the same way that it proved possible to abolish smallpox and painful surgery,[186] it is much more likely

---

[184] Cf. Pearce, 2017 and https://www.abolitionist.com/

[185] And this disagreement is in fact a profound philosophical one, as it ties deeply into
questions concerning what the nature of consciousness is, as well as what kinds of things that exist in the world. The following are some resources that present and discuss the different views in question:
https://www.physicalism.com/
https://foundational-research.org/the-eliminativist-approach-to-consciousness/
http://opentheory.net/2017/07/why-i-think-the-foundational-research-institute-should-rethink-its-approach/
https://www.utilitarianism.com/magnus-vinding/consciousness-realism.html
See also Brian Tomasik's explanation of why his focus differs from that of David Pearce:
http://reducing-suffering.org/dont-focus-hedonistic-imperative/

[186] Cf. https://www.general-anaesthesia.com/

that the persistence of human civilization will reduce rather than increase future suffering. On the other hand, if Brian Tomasik is right in believing suffering to be something of a more abstract nature, and something that cannot be abolished like smallpox could, this would seem to imply that the persistence of human civilization is most likely to vastly increase future suffering.[187] (Yet it should be noted that David Pearce, Brian Tomasik, and the Foundational Research Institute all unanimously oppose efforts to destroy the world, for reasons such as those provided above.)

Thus, our priorities depend critically on the answers we provide to these open questions pertaining to the reduction of future suffering, which is why research on them should be made a priority: so that we can provide more, and more detailed answers than the tentative and incomplete ones presented here.

I should like to conclude this chapter by re-emphasizing a tragic fact that is all too easily forgotten by our wishful and optimistic minds, that fact being that the world we inhabit is hopelessly far from Omelas. For our world is unfortunately nothing like a near-paradisiacal city predicated on the misery of a single starving child. Rather, in our world, there are millions of starving children, and millions of children who die from such starvation or otherwise readily preventable causes, every single year. And none of this misery serves to support a paradise or anything close to it. We do not live in a world where a starving child confined to a basement comprises anywhere near the worst forms of suffering that exist. Sadly, our world contains an incomprehensibly larger number of horrors of incomprehensibly greater severity, forms of suffering that make the sufferer wish dearly for a fate as "lucky" as that of the unfortunate child in

---

[187] At the moment of writing, Tomasik assigns a 69 percent credence to the claim "Human-inspired colonization of space will cause more suffering than it prevents if it happens", cf. http://reducing-suffering.org/summary-beliefs-values-big-questions/

Omelas. This is, of course, true even if we only consider the human realm, yet it is even more true if we also, as we must, consider the realm of non-human individuals. Humanity subjects billions of land-living individuals to conditions similar to those of the child in Omelas, and we inflict extreme suffering upon a significant fraction of them, by castrating them without anesthetics, boiling them alive, suffocating them, grinding them alive, etc. And our sins toward aquatic animals are even greater still, as we kill them in *far* greater numbers, trillions on some estimates, and, most tragically, these deaths probably involve extreme suffering more often than not, as we slowly drag these beings out of the deep, suffocate them, and cut off their heads without stunning or mercy. And yet even this horror story of unfathomable scale still falls hopelessly short of capturing the true extent of suffering in the world, as the suffering created by humanity only comprises a fraction of the totality of suffering on the planet, the vast majority of which is found in the wild, where non-human animals suffer and die from starvation, parasitism, and disease, not to mention being eaten alive, a source of extreme suffering for countless beings on the planet every single second.

Sadly, our condition is very far from Omelas indeed, implying that if one would choose to walk away from Omelas, it seems impossible to defend supporting the spread of our condition, or anything remotely like it, beyond Earth; or even to defend not making a dedicated effort to improve our present condition as it is. Indeed, no matter what values one may subscribe to, it is undeniable that the extent of suffering in the world is immense and overshadowing, and our future priorities should reflect this reality.

A GOOD LIFE: THE PRECONDITION
FOR EFFECTIVE ALTRUISM

In this final chapter I shall like to briefly address a tempting pitfall related to effective altruism — failing to invest sufficiently in oneself. For as noted in the introduction, effective altruism is not altruism in the irresponsible sense of sacrificing for others without any regard for oneself. Not only would that amount to an indefensible neglect of an individual of immense inherent value, i.e. the altruist, but it is also just an ineffective and unsustainable strategy for helping others. Indeed, effective altruism necessitates self-care of the highest quality.

For if one believes one is able to make a significant difference in the world, then one must also believe that one is worth investing the required resources into in order to make this difference-making possible. Self-investment is a precondition for making a difference. And such an investment might in fact be among the best investments one can possibly make as an altruist, as the impact of many of our actions are often highly unclear, whereas many of us can be quite sure that our future selves will be dedicated to the mission of helping others[188] (given our track record, pledges, peers, etc.), as well as presumably knowing more about how to pursue this mission than our present selves do. With extreme suffering crying out for alleviation every single second, it can, of course, seem

---

[188] I am grateful to Rubí Amoros for helping me see this point.

trivial and out of place to suggest that the best thing one can do might be to brush one's teeth carefully and change one's sheets. Yet, as counter-intuitive as such a suggestion is, it is quite likely true, at least occasionally. Such basic elements of self-care are essential for effective altruism, not trivial. As effective altruist Robert Wiblin has been quoted as saying, altruism is a marathon, not a sprint. Indeed, real-life effective altruism is not akin to heroically jumping into a pond to save a child once in a lifetime (although it may include that), but rather a matter of living a healthy and productive life guided by reflection and evidence, over the long haul.

Consider it this way: of all the altruistic projects you can undertake in your lifetime, how likely is it that the one you are currently working on is the most important of them all? Or more relevantly, how likely is it that it is more important than all the other projects you can do for the rest of your life combined? Unlikely, it seems safe to say. The importance of the project one happens to focus on at any given moment, especially early in one's career, is all but surely dwarfed by the importance of all future projects combined, which suggests that the goal of taking good care of oneself in a sustainable way that steers one clear of burnout should take precedence over the altruistic project one is working on. That minimizing "personal existential risks" should be a prime priority. And this conclusion likely holds true even if the project one is working on indeed is more important than all future projects combined, not least because this most important project itself likely only benefits from the proper self-care of its creator.

This conclusion is perhaps not one that helps us signal a willingness for self-sacrifice particularly well. Yet it is nonetheless a conclusion that holds true if we want to help others: we have to take very good care of ourselves, in a long-term fashion.

How Can We Best Help Ourselves?

So how is this best done? Well, we probably all know the most basic answer, which is all those boring things that wise people have been telling us about since the dawn of time: eat well, sleep well, exercise well, and, of course, limit the time you spend on social media (avoid addictions). These things are all crucial and should be made a top priority.

Yet there is, of course, more to living a healthy and productive life than merely eating and sleeping well, and this more advanced, level 2-stage of the good life has in fact also been covered quite well by advice from ancient folks, advice whose utility modern psychology now seems to confirm. Of such ancient advice, I find the Hindu concept of Puruṣārtha, or at least my own secular interpretation of it outlined below, a particularly clear and useful framework, yet one can readily find similar ideas in other traditions, as well as in recent books on positive psychology. Puruṣārtha means "object of human pursuit", and refers to what is considered the four proper goals of human life in the Hindu tradition, the necessary and sufficient goals for a good and fulfilling life.

The first of these goals is Dharma, which is basically about being a good, ethical person, but in all senses of the word. It is not enough to merely donate money to charity, even the most effective ones, or to do altruistically important research. One must also be a kind and respectful person, to others and oneself (which being a "good person" in the large-scale utilitarian sense just invoked certainly does not guarantee) — a person who seeks to live virtuously and in accordance with the local duties and laws necessary for social life to function. It is about living up to one's ethical responsibility in the broadest sense. And this would include, it is worth noting in this context, having the decency and compassion to not succumb to "effective altruist snobbery" in the form of looking down upon or mocking supposedly ineffective ways of helping (that may in fact do a great deal of good upon closer inspection), or deriding problems or misery because they may not seem of the very worst kind. No matter how much extreme suffering there is in the world, it does not change the intrinsic badness of the distress of a single homeless person, nor the fact that their distress is tragic and lamentable. To scorn at suffering and squalor, or at genuine attempts to help alleviate such misfortune, is not effective altruism, but merely a display of a lack of respect and empathetic understanding.

Simply put, Dharma is just all those things our elders taught us to do. The embodiment of the decency, responsibility, and goodness that not only makes life good for others around us, but which also tends to be deeply satisfying to ourselves. For instance, rather than being a personal sacrifice, giving to as well as doing things for others has been found to promote the happiness of the benefactor too.[189] But it is also satisfying in that the striving to live a responsible and ethical life can give us the feeling that we are living in a socially sustainable way that is in alignment with our own deepest values. And, not least, it can fulfill our need to contribute and give our lives meaning. Perhaps the deepest meaning possible.

Second, there is Artha, which is about having the basic means of life in order. It is about having a satisfying career and financial security, which enables one to live with a sense of safety, direction, and opportunities, but it is also about having one's home, belongings, and daily rhythm and routine in order, keeping things clean and functional. Essential stuff.

Yet being an ethical person with a good career and an orderly home is not enough, of course. We humans are social animals who have deep needs beyond merely being paragons of virtue and career success. We also have needs for social and sensual connection, and this is the dimension of life covered by the concept of Kama (as in "Kama Sutra", yes). Like Dharma, Kama is also a very broad notion, one that stands for pleasure, but of many sorts. It is about desire, lust, and pleasures of the senses, but it

---

[189] Dunn et al, 2008; Dunn et al, 2010; Mogensen, 2011.

is also about the enjoyment of life more generally, as well as the deep loving connections we have with friends and lovers. It is about having a soulmate, or many if one prefers, with whom one can share things openly and honestly, and who can provide comfort and support. It is about the importance of pleasure, in all its guises, for a good, fulfilling life.

Lastly, there is Moksha, which means liberation or release from suffering. In some schools of Hinduism, this concept has strong superstitious connotations, but in others, as well as in the secular interpretation proposed here, it simply refers to the self-knowledge and freedom from suffering that one can attain via spiritual practice, where "spiritual" is just a synonym for "meditative" or "contemplative". Such freedom may be brought about via yoga, meditation, or psychedelic drugs. For some it may just take a quiet walk.

In other words, Moksha, as interpreted here, basically refers to a tranquilist cleaning practice of throwing away, or at least detaching from, mental noise, including the often all too burdensome load of "the self", and then being left with an untroubled state, even as thoughts and temptations come and go. For many of us, such a practice is also a crucial part of the good life — a life with less stress and anxiety, as well as more happiness and resilience. Indeed, as a large meta-analysis of studies on mindfulness meditation found: "[Mindfulness-based therapy] is an effective treatment for a variety of psychological problems, and is especially effective for reducing anxiety, depression, and stress."[190]

Now, are these four things above all strictly necessary for everybody in order to live a good life? The answer, of course, depends on what we mean by "a good life", but if we merely mean a life that the person who lives it finds satisfying, then clearly not. Human beings vary a lot, and many seem able to live happy lives in the absence of some of the elements above.

---

[190] Khoury et al, 2013.

Interestingly, it actually seems that some of the above-mentioned aims in life can serve as substitutes for each other, at least with respect to the end of a happy personal life. For example, some people have dropped their careers and social connections in order to live a contemplative life, a life animated chiefly by the aim of Moksha, and some of them appear perfectly happy with such a life. And other people may have so much "Kama", so much love and pleasure in life, that spiritual practice is of limited emotional value.

Nonetheless, I would argue that all four elements most likely are necessary, or at least helpful, for most of us in order to live a good life in the sense most worth striving for. For while it may be possible to live a personally satisfying life in meditative isolation, such a life does not seem aligned with that which, in my view, has the greatest value in the final analysis (cf. the foregoing chapters on values), namely Dharma: living an ethical life. More specifically, a life in which one reduces the greatest amount of extreme suffering. Such a life is unlikely to be one of isolated contemplation, but rather one of active involvement. A life in which we engage with the world, by being humble learners and responsible agents who learn and work toward its betterment in a manner consistent with financial security and career success. All the while being powered by, and enjoying, our most preferred and needed pleasures, connections, and meditative practices — whatever quality self-care that is required in order for us to have a fulfilling life that feels worth living, and without which there is no complete Dharma or effective altruism. Without which we cannot be the light that brightens the darkness of the world.

ACKNOWLEDGMENTS

I should like to thank David Pearce for encouraging me to write this book, and for providing comments and suggestions throughout the writing process. For all the things he has done for me, I owe David more thanks than I can ever express. I also want to thank Simon Knutsson for reading and commenting on parts of the book. David and Simon are not only supportive friends, but also intellectual inspirations who have influenced my views and the contents of this book significantly. I feel the same about Brian Tomasik, who also gave valuable feedback on the book, and whose writings, both public and private, have inspired, challenged, and consoled me a great deal over the last few years, for which I am very grateful. Indeed, beyond their personal support, David, Simon, and Brian all have my deepest gratitude for their immeasurably important work.

I should also like to thank Jonathan Leighton, both for the important and inspiring work he does to prevent extreme suffering, as well as for carefully reading and commenting on a draft. Two other great inspirations of mine I must thank for reading and commenting extensively on a draft — and not least for their important work to help other sentient beings — are Oscar Horta and Lara André.

I thank Cynthia M. Stewart for proofreading and commenting with a degree of thoroughness, expedience, and dedication that exceeded all reasonable expectation. Cynthia's touch benefited the book immensely. I am also grateful to the following people for providing valuable feedback: David Althaus, Jan Beck, Robert Daoust, Ben Davidow, Manu Herrán, Thomas Richards, Sebastian Simon Sudergaard Schmidt, Peter Singer, and Katie Willis.

My work on this book was in part funded by the Effective Altruism Foundation, although the views expressed herein are not necessarily endorsed by EAF. I am grateful to all the people whom I have engaged with at EAF, especially Daniel Kestenholz, Max Daniel, and David Althaus who have been my main points of contact at EAF. It is a privilege to be among a circle of such remarkable people who continually leave me feeling humbled and impressed. More than that, EAF has also, especially by virtue of the conferences it has organized, been a main facilitator for bringing me in touch with most of the like-minded people I now know. Tribal and primitive as it may be, I feel that EAF in many ways has served as the key linchpin for "my people", for which we are many who owe it our thanks.

Finally, I want to send deep thanks to my friends Joachim, Ailin, Magnus, Joe, and Jess for making my life such a joy, and to Sille, for carefully reading a draft and providing valuable comments, and, most of all, for being such a bright and warm light in a world that contains so much horror and tragedy.

BIBLIOGRAPHY

Althaus, D. & Gloor, L. (2016). Reducing Risks of Astronomical Suffering: A Neglected Priority. *foundational-research.com*. Retrieved from: https://foundational-research.org/reducing-risks-of-astronomical-suffering-a-neglected-priority/

Animal Ethics. (2012/2016). Speciesism. *animal-ethics.org*. Retrieved from: http://www.animal-ethics.org/speciesism/

Animal Ethics. (2013/2016). Working for a future with fewer harms to wild animals. *animal-ethics.org*. Retrieved from: http://www.animal-ethics.org/wild-animal-suffering-section/helping-animals-in-the-wild/working-for-a-future-with-fewer-harms-to-wild-animals/

Aristotle., Ross, W. & Brown, L. (350 BC/2009). *The Nicomachean Ethics*. Oxford New York: Oxford University Press.

Balcombe, J. (2006/2007). *Pleasurable Kingdom: Animals and the Nature of Feeling Good*. Basingstoke: Macmillan.

Bastardi, A., Uhlmann, E. L., Ross, L. (2011). Wishful Thinking: Belief, Desire, and the Motivated Evaluation of Scientific Evidence. *Psychological Science*. 22(6), pp. 731-732.

Bastian, B., Loughnan, S., Haslam, N., Radke, H., (2012). Don't Mind Meat? The Denial of Mind to Animals Used for Human Consumption. *Personality and Social Psychology Bulletin*, 38 (2) pp. 247-256. Retrieved from: http://journals.sagepub.com/doi/abs/10.1177/0146167211424291

Baumann, T. (2016). Why Wild Animals? *was-research.org*. Retrieved from: https://was-research.org/mission/

Baumann, T. (2017a). Should altruists prioritize the far future? *prioritizationresearch.com*. Retrieved from: http://prioritizationresearch.com/should-altruists-prioritize-the-far-future/

Baumann, T. (2017b). Should altruists focus on artificial intelligence? *prioritizationresearch.com*. Retrieved from: http://prioritizationresearch.com/should-altruists-focus-on-artificial-intelligence/

Baumann, T. (2017c). Arguments for and against moral advocacy. *prioritizationresearch.com*. Retrieved from: http://prioritizationresearch.com/arguments-for-and-against-moral-advocacy/

Baumann, T. (2017d). Uncertainty smoothes out differences in impact. *prioritizationresearch.com*. Retrieved from: http://prioritizationresearch.com/uncertainty-smoothes-out-differences-in-impact/

Baumann, T. (2017e). S-risks: An introduction. *s-risk.org*. Retrieved from: http://s-risks.org/intro/

Baumann, T. (2017f). S-risk FAQ. *s-risk.org.* Retrieved from:
http://s-risks.org/faq/

Beckstead, N. (2013). On the Overwhelming Importance of the Far Future (PhD thesis). Retrieved from:
https://rucore.libraries.rutgers.edu/rutgers-lib/40469/PDF/1/play/

Bekoff, M. (2007). *Animals Matter: A Biologist Explains Why We Should Treat Animals with Compassion and Respect.* Boston New York: Shambhala Distributed in the United States by Random House.

Benatar, D. (2006). *Better Never to Have Been: The Harm of Coming into Existence.* Oxford New York: Clarendon Press Oxford University Press.

Bentham, J. (1789/2007). *An Introduction to the Principles of Morals and Legislation.* Mineola, N.Y: Dover Publications.

Berridge, K.C. & Kringelbach, M.L. (2011). Building a neuroscience of pleasure and well-being. *Psychol Well Being.* 1(1), pp. 1-3.

Bertrand, O. (2016). Reducing suffering or adding years of life? Effective altruism and divergences in value judgments and worldviews. Presented at the 14th Conference of the International Society for Utilitarian Studies. Retrieved from:
https://www.academia.edu/26705132/Reducing_suffering_or_adding_years_of_life_Effective_a
ltruism_and_divergences_in_value_judgments_and_worldviews

Beshkar, M. (2008). The presence of consciousness in the absence of the cerebral cortex. *Synapse.* 62 (7), pp. 553-556.

Bostrom, N. (2013). Existential Risk Prevention as Global Priority. *Global Policy,* 4 (1) pp. 15-31. Retrieved from:
http://www.existential-risk.org/concept.pdf

Bostrom, N. (2014). *Superintelligence: paths, dangers, strategies.* Oxford, United Kingdom: Oxford University Press.

Brülde, B. (2010). Happiness, Morality, and Politics. *Journal of Happiness Studies,* 11, pp. 567-83.

Camus, A. & Gilbert, S. (1947/1991). *The Plague.* New York: Vintage Books, a division of Random House, Inc.

Carey, R. (2015). *The Effective Altruism Handbook.* Centre For Effective Altruism, Oxford, Oxfordshire United Kingdom.

Caviola, L. [Effective Altruism Global] (2017, November). Against Naive Effective Altruism | Lucius Caviola | EAGxBerlin 2017. Retrieved from:
https://www.youtube.com/watch?v=-2oRgxxafXk

Caviola, L., Everett, J.A., & Faber, N.S. (2018). The Moral Standing of Animals: Towards a Psychology of Speciesism. *Journal of Personality and Social Psychology.* Retrieved from:
https://psyarxiv.com/m5cwq

Churchland, P. (2011). *Braintrust: What Neuroscience Tells Us about Morality.* Princeton, N.J: Princeton University Press.

Damasio, A. (1994/2005). *Descartes' Error: Emotion, Reason, and the Human Brain.* London New York: Penguin.

Darwin, C. (1872). *The Expression of Emotion in Man and Animals*. Oxford, England: Appleton

Davidow, B. (2013). Why Most People Don't Care About Wild-Animal Suffering. *reducing-suffering.org*. Retrieved from:
http://reducing-suffering.org/why-most-people-dont-care-about-wild-animal-suffering/

Dawkins, R. (1976/2006). *The Selfish Gene*. Oxford New York: Oxford University Press.

Dawkins, R. (2011). Richard Dawkins on vivisection: "But can they suffer?". *boingboing.net*. Retrieved from:
http://boingboing.net/2011/06/30/richard-dawkins-on-v.html

Donaldson, S. & Kymlicka, W. (2011). *Zoopolis: A Political Theory of Animal Rights*. Oxford England New York: Oxford University Press.

Dunayer, J. (2001). *Animal Equality: Language and Liberation*. Derwood, Md: Ryce Pub.

Dunn, E.W., Aknin, L.B., Norton, M.I. (2008). Spending Money on Others Promotes Happiness. *Science*, 319 (5870), pp. 1687-1688. Retrieved from:
https://greatergood.berkeley.edu/images/application_uploads/norton-spendingmoney.pdf

Dunn, E.W., Gilbert, D.T., Wilson, T.D. (2010). If money doesn't make you happy, then you probably aren't spending it right. *Journal of Consumer Psychology*, 21 (2011), pp. 115-125. Retrieved from:
http://www.danielgilbert.com/DUNN%20GILBERT%20&%20WILSON%20(2011).pdf

Effective Altruism Foundation. (2016). The Importance of the Far Future. Retrieved from:
https://ea-foundation.org/blog/the-importance-of-the-far-future/

Faria, C. & Paez, E. (2015). Animals in need: The problem of wild animal suffering and intervention in nature. *Relations: Beyond Anthropocentrism*, 3, pp.7-13. Retrieved from:
http://www.ledonline.it/index.php/Relations/article/view/816/660

Fehige, C. (1998). A pareto principle for possible people. In Fehige, C. and Wessels U. (Eds.), *Preferences*, pp. 508-43. Berlin: Walter de Gruyter.

Francione, G.L. (1999/2011). *Introduction to Animal Rights: Your Child or the Dog?* Temple University Press.

Gloor, L. & Mannino, A. (2015). Negative Utilitarianism FAQ. *utilitarianism.com*. Retrieved from:
https://www.utilitarianism.com/nu/nufaq.html

Gloor, L. & Mannino, A. (2016). The Case for Suffering-Focused Ethics. *foundational-research.com*. Retrieved from:
https://foundational-research.org/the-case-for-suffering-focused-ethics/

Gloor, L. (2016). Altruists Should Prioritize Artificial Intelligence. *foundational-research.com*. Retrieved from:
https://foundational-research.org/altruists-should-prioritize-artificial-intelligence/

Gloor, L. (2017). Tranquilism. *foundational-research.com*. Retrieved from:
https://foundational-research.org/tranquilism/

Gloor, L. (2018). Cause prioritization for downside-focused value systems. *foundational-research.com*. Retrieved from:
https://foundational-research.org/cause-prioritization-downside-focused-value-systems/

Griffin, D.R., Speck, G.B. (2004). New evidence of animal consciousness. *Anim Cogn.* 7(1), pp. 5-18.

Guin, U. (1973/1993). *The Ones Who Walk Away from Omelas.* Mankato, Minn: Creative Education.

Harris, S. (2004/2005). *The End of Faith: Religion, Terror, and the Future of Reason.* New York: W.W. Norton & Co.

Harris, S. (2010/2011). *The Moral Landscape: How Science Can Determine Human Values.* New York: Free Press.

Holtug, N. (2004). Person-affecting Moralities. In Jesper Ryberg and Torbjörn Tännsjö, eds., *The Repugnant Conclusion.* Dordrecht: Kluwer. pp. 129-61.

Horta, O. (2010a). Debunking the Idyllic View of Natural Processes: Population Dynamics and Suffering in the Wild. *Télos.* 17, pp. 73-88. Retrieved from: https://masalladelaespecie.files.wordpress.com/2012/05/debunkingidyllicviewhorta.pdf

Horta, O. (2010b). What Is Speciesism?. *Journal of Agricultural and Environmental Ethics.* 23, pp. 243-66. Retrieved from: https://masalladelaespecie.files.wordpress.com/2010/05/whatisspeciesism.pdf

Horta, O. [EffectiveAltruismCH] (2013, May). Oscar Horta: Why animal suffering is overwhelmingly prevalent in nature. Retrieved from: https://www.youtube.com/watch?v=cZ0XTofuGmY

Horta, O. [Jean Pierre Froud] (2013, September). Oscar Horta - About Strategies. Retrieved from: https://www.youtube.com/watch?v=v_vsHlKZPFQ

Horta, O. (2014). Egalitarianism and Animals. *Between the Species*, 19(1), pp. 109-145.

Hume, D. (1751/2012). *An Enquiry Concerning the Principles of Morals.* Lexington, Ky: Maestro Reprints.

Inmendham [CrownJules84]. (2013, February). Gladiator War (Graphic Content). Retrieved from: https://www.youtube.com/watch?v=bK2a-1K0Sdg&t=8s

Inmendham [graytaich0]. (2011-2015). Best Work. Youtube playlist by graytaich0. Retrieved from: https://www.youtube.com/watch?v=b1mJnEmjlLE&list=PLcmZ9oxph4sxzDfr2oH6tpNij-YUH5dy3

Jabr, F. (2018). It's Official: Fish Feel Pain. *Smithsonian Magazine.* Retrieved from: https://www.smithsonianmag.com/science-nature/fish-feel-pain-180967764/

James W. (1901). Letter on happiness to Miss Frances R. Morse. In: James H, editor. Letters of William James. Vol. 2. Boston: Atlantic Monthly Press; 1920.

Johnson, M. (2017). Why I think the Foundational Research Institute should rethink its approach. *opentheory.net.* Retrieved from: http://opentheory.net/2017/07/why-i-think-the-foundational-research-institute-should-rethink-its-approach/

Karnofsky, H. (2011). Why we can't take expected value estimates literally (even when they're unbiased). The GiveWell Blog. Retrieved from: https://blog.givewell.org/2011/08/18/why-we-cant-take-expected-value-estimates-literally-even-when-theyre-unbiased/

Karnofsky, H. (2014). Sequence thinking vs. cluster thinking. The GiveWell Blog. Retrieved from:
https://blog.givewell.org/2014/06/10/sequence-thinking-vs-cluster-thinking/

Khoury, B. et al. (2013). Mindfulness-based therapy: A comprehensive meta-analysis. *Clinical Psychology Review,* 33 (6) pp. 763-771. Retrieved from:
https://www.sciencedirect.com/science/article/pii/S0272735813000731

Knutsson, S. (2015a/2016). The 'Asymmetry' and Extinction Thought Experiments. *foundational-research.org.* Retrieved from:
https://foundational-research.org/the-asymmetry-and-extinction-thought-experiments/

Knutsson, S. (2015b/2016). The Seriousness of Suffering: Supplement. Retrieved from:
http://www.simonknutsson.com/the-seriousness-of-suffering-supplement

Knutsson, S. (2016a/2017). How Could an Empty World Be Better than a Populated One? *foundational-research.org.* Retrieved from:
https://foundational-research.org/how-could-an-empty-world-be-better-than-a-populated/

Knutsson, S. (2016b/2017). Measuring Happiness and Suffering. *foundational-research.org.* Retrieved from:
https://foundational-research.org/measuring-happiness-and-suffering/

Knutsson, S. (2016c). Reducing Suffering Amongst Invertebrates Such As Insects. *was-research.org.* Retrieved from:
https://was-research.org/writing-by-others/reducing-suffering-amongst-invertebrates-insects/

Knutsson, S. (2016d). What Is the Difference Between Weak Negative and Non-Negative Ethical Views? *foundational-research.org.* Retrieved from:
https://foundational-research.org/what-is-the-difference-between-weak-negative-and-non-negative-ethical-views/

Knutsson, S. (2016e). Thoughts on Ord's "Why I'm Not a Negative Utilitarian". Retrieved from:
http://www.simonknutsson.com/thoughts-on-ords-why-im-not-a-negative-utilitarian

Knutsson, S. (2016f). Value Lexicality. *foundational-research.org.* Retrieved from:
https://foundational-research.org/value-lexicality/

Knutsson, S. [Foundational Research Institute] (2017, April). Simon Knutsson – Suffering-Focused Ethics and Effective Altruism. Retrieved from:
https://www.youtube.com/watch?v=2CfBcHii06w

Knutsson, S. (2017a). A Virtue of Precaution Regarding the Moral Status of Animals with Uncertain Sentience. *foundational-research.org.* Retrieved from:
https://foundational-research.org/virtue-precaution-regarding-moral-status-animals-uncertain-sentience/

Knutsson, S. (2017b). The World Destruction Argument. Unpublished working paper. Retrieved from:
http://www.simonknutsson.com/the-world-destruction-argument/

Leighton, J. (2011). *The Battle for Compassion: Ethics in an Apathetic Universe.* New York: Algora Pub.

Leighton, J. [Jonathan Leighton] (2015, March). The Battle for Compassion - a short film by Jonathan Leighton. Retrieved from:
https://www.youtube.com/watch?v=DBiKl_v5Mls

Leighton, J. [Jonathan Leighton] (2017, January). Guided Meditation for Activists. Retrieved from:
https://www.youtube.com/watch?v=D2YZew3Knj8

Leighton, J. (2017). Thriving in the Age of Factory Farming. *medium.com*. Retrieved from:
https://medium.com/@jonleighton1/thriving-in-the-age-of-factory-farming-fbcca7121d67

Low, P., Panksepp, J., Reiss, D., Edelman, D., Swinderen, B.V., & Koch, C. (2012). The Cambridge Declaration on Consciousness. Retrieved from:
http://fcmconference.org/img/CambridgeDeclarationOnConsciousness.pdf

MacAskill, W. (2015). *Doing Good Better: How Effective Altruism Can Help You Make a Difference*. New York, N.Y: Gotham Books.

MacAskill, W. (2017). Effective Altruism: Introduction. *Essays in Philosophy*, 18(1), pp. 1-5. Retrieved from:
http://dx.doi.org/10.7710/1526-0569.1580

Mannino, A. & Donnelly, R. [frei denken uni basel]. (2014, January). Reducing Wild Animal Suffering. Retrieved from:
https://www.youtube.com/watch?v=4aa6g1y4l8I

Mannino, A. [TEDx Talks]. (2014, February). Our daily life and death decisions: Adriano Mannino at TEDxGundeldingen. Retrieved from:
https://www.youtube.com/watch?v=-4rh5L4iluw

Mannino, A. (2015). Effective donation: Why you can save many more animals with your wallet than with your plate. *sentience-politics.com*. Retrieved from:
https://sentience-politics.org/effective-donation

Mannino, A. [Sentience Politics] (2015, March). Adriano Mannino: Effective Altruism for All Sentient Beings. Retrieved from:
https://www.youtube.com/watch?v=rFPqBJewI60

Mannino, A. [Talks at Google] (2017, August). Adriano Mannino: "Effective Altruism" | Talks at Google. Retrieved from:
https://www.youtube.com/watch?v=-lkrb20YGYw

Mayerfeld, J. (1999). *Suffering and Moral Responsibility*. New York Oxford: Oxford University Press.

Mill, J. S. (1863/2007). *Utilitarianism*. Mineola, N.Y: Dover Publications.

Mogensen, A. (2011). Giving Without Sacrifice? The relationship between income, happiness, and giving. Giving What We Can Research. Retrieved from:
https://www.givingwhatwecan.org/sites/givingwhatwecan.org/files/attachments/giving-without-sacrifice.pdf

Moor, M. [TEDx Talks]. (2013, December). Impact through rationality. Retrieved from:
https://www.youtube.com/watch?v=PcWus1943K0

Narveson, J. (1973). Moral problems of population. *The Monist*, 57 (1), 62-86.

Ng, Y-K. (1995). Towards Welfare Biology: Evolutionary Economics of Animal Consciousness and Suffering. *Biology and Philosophy*. 10, pp. 255-85. Retrieved from:
http://www.stafforini.com/library/ng-1995.pdf

Parfit, D. (1984/1987). *Reasons and Persons*. Oxford Oxfordshire: Clarendon Press.

Pearce, D. (1995/2007). *The Hedonistic Imperative*. Published online at:
http://www.hedweb.com/hedab.htm

Pearce, D. (1997). Review of "The Conscious Mind" by David Chalmers. Retrieved from:
https://www.hedweb.com/philsoph/chalmers.htm

Pearce, D. (2005). The Pinprick Argument. *utilitarianism.org*. Retrieved from:
http://utilitarianism.org/pinprick-argument.html

Pearce, D. (2007). The Abolitionist Project. *abolitionist.com*. Retrieved from:
https://www.abolitionist.com/

Pearce, D. (2009). Reprogramming Predators. *hedweb.com*. Retrieved from:
http://www.hedweb.com/abolitionist-project/reprogramming-predators.html

Pearce, D. (2012). The Anti-Speciesist Revolution. *hedweb.com*. Retrieved from:
https://www.hedweb.com/transhumanism/antispeciesist.html

Pearce, D. [Adam Ford]. (2013, February). David Pearce - Effective Altruism - Phasing
Out Suffering. Retrieved from:
https://www.youtube.com/watch?v=Yym0VzgXBGk

Pearce, D. [Foundational Research Institute] (2014/2015, January). David Pearce on
abolishing suffering. Retrieved from:
https://www.youtube.com/watch?v=_VCb9sk6CTc&t=2580s

Pearce, D. (2014/2016). Non-Materialist Physicalism: An experimentally testable
conjecture. *physicalism.com*. Retrieved from:
https://www.physicalism.com/

Pearce, D. (2017). *Can Biotechnology Abolish Suffering?* North Carolina: The Neuroethics
Foundation.

Pinker, S. (2002). *The Blank Slate: The Modern Denial of Human Nature*. New York:
Penguin.

Plous, S. (1993). *The Psychology of Judgment and Decision Making*. New York: McGraw-
Hill.

Popper, K. (1945/2011). *The Open Society and Its Enemies*. London: Routledge.

Putnam, H. (2002). *The Collapse of the Fact/Value Dichotomy and Other Essays*.
Cambridge, MA: Harvard University Press.

Putnam, H. [SonytoBratsoni]. (2012, May). The Fact/Value Dichotomy and its critics -
Hilary Putnam. Retrieved from:
https://www.youtube.com/watch?v=wCTawI5hfEU

Rawls, J. & Kelly, E. (2001). *Justice as Fairness: A Restatement*. Cambridge, Mass:
Harvard University Press.

Ray, G. (2017). How many neurons are there? *eukaryotewritesblog.com*. Retrieved from:
https://eukaryotewritesblog.com/how-many-neurons-are-there/

Reese, J. (2018). Why I prioritize moral circle expansion over artificial intelligence
alignment. Effective Altruism Forum. Retrieved from:
http://effective-altruism.com/ea/1l0/why_i_prioritize_moral_circle_expansion_over/

Regan, T. (1983/2004). *The Case for Animal Rights*. Berkeley: University of California
Press.

Schopenhauer, A. & Hollingdale, R. (1970). *Essays and Aphorisms*. Harmondsworth, Eng: Penguin Books.

Sentience Politics. (2016a). Invertebrate Suffering. *sentience-politics.com*. Retrieved from: https://sentience-politics.org/research/policy-papers/invertebrate-suffering/

Sentience Politics. (2016b). The Case Against Speciesism. *sentience-politics.com*. Retrieved from: https://sentience-politics.org/philosophy/the-case-against-speciesism/

Sidgwick, H. (1874/1981). *The Methods of Ethics*. Indianapolis: Hackett Pub. Co.

Simler, K. & Hanson, R. (2018). *The Elephant in the Brain: Hidden Motives in Everyday Life*. New York, NY: Oxford University Press.

Singer, P. (1972). Famine, Affluence, and Morality. *Philosophy and Public Affairs*, 1(1), pp. 229-243. Revised edition retrieved from: https://www.utilitarian.net/singer/by/1972----.htm

Singer, P. (1980a/2011). *Practical Ethics*. New York: Cambridge University Press.

Singer, P. (1980b). Right to Life? *The New York Review of Books*. Retrieved from: http://www.nybooks.com/articles/1980/08/14/right-to-life/

Singer, P. (1997). The Drowning Child and the Expanding Circle Peter Singer. New Internationalist. Retrieved from: https://www.utilitarian.net/singer/by/199704--.htm

Singer, P. (2015). *The Most Good You Can Do: How Effective Altruism Is Changing Ideas About Living Ethically*. New Haven London: Yale University Press.

Singer, P. (2016). Are Insects Conscious? *project-syndicate.org*. Retrieved from: https://www.project-syndicate.org/commentary/are-insects-conscious-by-peter-singer-2016-05?barrier=accessreg

Sinick, J. (2013). Some reservations about Singer's child-in-the-pond argument. *lesswrong.com*. http://lesswrong.com/lw/hr5/some_reservations_about_singers_childinthepond/

Slovic, P. (2007). "If I look at the mass I will never act": Psychic numbing and genocide. *Judgment and Decision Making*. 2(2), pp. 79-95.

Smart, R.N. (1958). Negative Utilitarianism. *Mind*. 67, pp. 542-543.

Speciesism: The Movie. (2012). Film. Directed by Mark Devries. Mark Devries Productions.

Szabó, L. (2003). Formal System as Physical Objects: A Physicalist Account of Mathematical Truth. *International Studies in the Philosophy of Science*, 17, 117-125. Retrieved from:
http://www.tandfonline.com/doi/pdf/10.1080/0269859031000160568?needAccess=true

Tenney, E.R., Poole, J. M., Diener, E. (2016). Does positivity enhance work performance?: Why, when, and what we don't know. *Research in Organizational Behavior* 36. Retrieved from: https://www.researchgate.net/publication/309878713_Does_positivity_enhance_work_performance_Why_when_and_what_we_don't_know

Todd, B. (2015). Why you should focus more on talent gaps, not funding gaps. *80000hours.org*. Retrieved from:
https://80000hours.org/2015/11/why-you-should-focus-more-on-talent-gaps-not-funding-gaps/

Todd, B. (2016a). Tech startup founder. *80000hours.org*. Retrieved from:
https://80000hours.org/career-reviews/tech-entrepreneurship/

Todd, B. (2016b). *80,000 Hours: Find a fulfilling career that does good*. Oxford: Centre for Effective Altruism.

Todd, B. (2016c). How much do hedge fund traders earn? *80000hours.org*. Retrieved from:
https://80000hours.org/2017/05/how-much-do-hedge-fund-traders-earn/

Tomasik, B. (2006/2016). On the Seriousness of Suffering. *utilitarian-essays.com*. Retrieved from:
http://reducing-suffering.org/on-the-seriousness-of-suffering/

Tomasik, B. (2007/2016). Why Maximize Expected Value?. *utilitarian-essays.com*. Retrieved from:
http://reducing-suffering.org/why-maximize-expected-value/

Tomasik, B. (2009a/2014). Do Bugs Feel Pain? *utilitarian-essays.com*. Retrieved from:
http://reducing-suffering.org/do-bugs-feel-pain/

Tomasik, B. (2009b/2014). The Importance of Wild-Animal Suffering. *utilitarian-essays.com*. Retrieved from:
http://www.utilitarian-essays.com/suffering-nature.html

Tomasik, B. (2009c/2014). The Predominance of Wild-Animal Suffering over Happiness: An Open Problem. Retrieved from:
http://reducing-suffering.org/wp-content/uploads/2014/10/wild-animals.pdf

Tomasik, B. (2009d/2014). How Many Wild Animals Are There?. *reducing-suffering.org*. Retrieved from:
http://reducing-suffering.org/how-many-wild-animals-are-there/

Tomasik, B. (2011/2016). Risks of Astronomical Future Suffering. *foundational-research.org*. Retrieved from:
https://foundational-research.org/risks-of-astronomical-future-suffering/

Tomasik, B. (2012a/2016). Donating toward Efficient Online Veg Ads. *reducing-suffering.org*. Retrieved from:
http://reducing-suffering.org/donating-toward-efficient-online-veg-ads/

Tomasik, B. (2012b/2014). Suffering in Animals vs. Humans. *utilitarian-essays.com*. Retrieved from:
http://www.utilitarian-essays.com/suffering-in-animals-vs-humans.html

Tomasik, B. (2013a/2015). Against Wishful Thinking. foundational-research.org. Retrieved from:
https://foundational-research.org/against-wishful-thinking/

Tomasik, B. (2013b/2014). Speculations on Population Dynamics of Bug Suffering. *utilitarian-essays.com*. Retrieved from:
http://www.utilitarian-essays.com/bug-populations.html

Tomasik, B. (2013c/2014). Applied Welfare Biology and Why Wild-Animal Advocates Should Focus on Not Spreading Nature. *utilitarian-essays.com*. Retrieved from:
http://www.utilitarian-essays.com/applied-welfare-biology.html

Tomasik, B. (2013d/2016). The Horror of Suffering. *utilitarian-essays.com*. Retrieved from:
http://reducing-suffering.org/the-horror-of-suffering/

Tomasik, B. (2013e). Education Matters for Altruism. *foundational-research.com*. Retrieved from:
https://foundational-research.org/education-matters-for-altruism/

Tomasik, B. (2014/2018). The Eliminativist Approach to Consciousness. *foundational-research.com*. Retrieved from:
https://foundational-research.org/the-eliminativist-approach-to-consciousness/

Tomasik, B. (2015a). The Importance of Insect Suffering. *utilitarian-essays.com*. Retrieved from:
http://reducing-suffering.org/the-importance-of-insect-suffering/

Tomasik, B. (2015b). Should Altruists Focus on Reducing Short-Term or Far-Future Suffering? *utilitarian-essays.com*. Retrieved from:
http://reducing-suffering.org/altruists-focus-reducing-short-term-far-future-suffering/

Tomasik, B. (2015c). Reasons to Promote Suffering-Focused Ethics. *utilitarian-essays.com*. Retrieved from:
http://reducing-suffering.org/the-case-for-promoting-suffering-focused-ethics/

Tomasik, B. [Brian Tomasik]. (2016, March). Preventing Extreme Suffering Has Moral Priority [graphic content in middle of video]. Retrieved from:
https://www.youtube.com/watch?v=RyA_eF7W02s

Unger, P. (1996). *Living High and Letting Die: Our Illusion of Innocence*. New York: Oxford University Press.

Vinding, M. (2014a). *Why We Should Go Vegan*.

Vinding, M. (2014b). *Why "Happy Meat" Is Always Wrong*.

Vinding, M. (2014c). *The Simple Case for Going Vegan*.

Vinding, M. (2014d). *A Copernican Revolution in Ethics*.

Vinding, M. (2014e). *Moral Truths: The Foundation of Ethics*.

Vinding, M. (2014f). *The Meaning of Life: An Examination of Purpose*.

Vinding, M. (2015a). *Speciesism: Why It Is Wrong and the Implications of Rejecting It*.

Vinding, M. (2015b). *Anti-Natalism and the Future of Suffering: Why Negative Utilitarians Should not Aim for Extinction*.

Vinding, M. (2015c). The Harm of Death. Retrieved from:
https://www.utilitarianism.com/magnus-vinding/harm-death.html

Vinding, M. (2016a). *The Speciesism of Leaving Nature Alone, and the Theoretical Case for "Wildlife Anti-Natalism"*.

Vinding, M. (2016b). Consciousness Realism: The Non-Eliminativist Physicalist View of Consciousness. Retrieved from:
https://www.utilitarianism.com/magnus-vinding/consciousness-realism.html

Vinding, M. (2016c). *Reflections on Intelligence*.

Vinding, M. (2016d). *Induction Is All We Got: Essays on Epistemology*.

Vinding, M. (2016e). Animal advocates should focus on antispeciesism, not veganism. Sentience Politics. Retrieved from:
https://sentience-politics.org/animal-advocates-focus-antispeciesism-not-veganism/

Vinding, M. (2017a). *What Should We Do?: Essays on Cause Prioritization and Fundamental Values.*

Vinding, M. (2017b). *You Are Them.*

Vinding, M. (2017c). Notes on the Utility of Anti-Speciesist Advocacy. Retrieved from: https://magnusvinding.com/2017/10/24/notes-on-the-utility-of-anti-speciesist-advocacy/

Vinding, M. (2017d). A Contra AI FOOM Reading List. Retrieved from: https://magnusvinding.com/2017/12/16/a-contra-ai-foom-reading-list/

Wiblin, R. (2017). What are the most important talent gaps in the effective altruism community? *80000hours.org.* Retrieved from: https://80000hours.org/2017/11/talent-gaps-survey-2017/

45803625R00082

Printed in Poland
by Amazon Fulfillment
Poland Sp. z o.o., Wrocław